VOLUNTARY SERVITUDE

Charles J. Levy

VOLUNTARY SERVITUDE

WHITES IN THE

NEGRO MOVEMENT

New York

APPLETON-CENTURY-CROFTS

Division of Meredith Corporation

PRINTED IN THE UNITED STATES OF AMERICA
E 55620

PREFACE

This exploration is an attempt to understand what happens when members of a dominant group seek membership in a dominated group; when, in addition, the admission requirements set by the dominated group are at least as insurmountable as those imposed on its members for entrance into the dominant group. For trust, which provided this explorer with a focus, is perhaps the one thing that members of a dominated group can withhold.

The research was experienced before it was initiated. Rather than impose a research topic on the Negro community, it was hoped the Negro community would impose a research topic. But first it seemed necessary to have a legitimized presence in the Negro community. Partly for this reason, four years (beginning 1963, and preceded by intermittent stays in the South) were spent on the faculty of a predominantly Negro college in the Deep South, while concurrently participating in a Southern-based civil rights organization. The Negro community did, in fact, impose the topic —by making it clear that a White cannot legitimize his presence in a Negro community.

The material is arranged in a sequence intended to approximate the stages through which Whites in the Movement pass as they move toward a recognition of the mistrust directed at them. Chapters, representing the successive stages, are presented in terms of the subjective reality that the Whites are undergoing. Where relevant, it is contrasted with the objective reality confronting them, that is, the subjective reality of the Negro.

Whites considered here to be in the Movement include not only civil rights workers, but also instructors and students at Negro colleges. There are undeniable differences between colleges and civil rights organizations. The most apparent substantive difference is that education tends to be an inherently traditional process, and thereby preserves the established order, while civil rights organizations are inherently committed to altering the established order. The most apparent procedural difference is that the Negro college has little autonomy, while the Southern-based civil rights organization has a considerable degree of it. But in spite of differences between the respective settings, there are few points at which the condition of Whites, and their reaction to it, do not overlap; often, they are indistinguishable.

For this reason, incidents reported here did not happen within any one civil rights organization or college; contact with several of each was drawn on for illustrations. The place of the White was essentially the same, regardless of whether the organization has a bourgeoise orientation or a proletarian one; or whether the college is, to use the distinction of a Negro student, "a house nigger's school," or "a field nigger's school." Accordingly, the college and the civil rights organization, respectively, are presented as amalgams.

The investigation mainly relied on unstructured participant observation, because whenever a more formal approach was used it created a variety of difficulties. One example arose when an assisting Negro student asked a classmate the following question during what was clearly an interview: "What would it be like if ——— had a White president?" The reply was: "Well, really, I don't think it would make much difference because I believe that ——— needs to be changed. Just because [a Negro] founded ——— doesn't mean that it has to be run by Negroes. Furthermore, I feel that a White President would change some of these rules of ——— that date back to antiquity." Later that week, a similar question came up during an informal discussion in the dormitory. This time the response, from the same student, was: "We don't want a White President! —— would be something like a plantation when he got the reins of it." (By itself, there is no indication that the second response is necessarily the more honest one, but the interviewer believed it was on the basis of her private relationship with the student.)

A more general problem developed from the fact that Negroes are apt to regard any research in their world that is undertaken by Whites as a form of "exploitation," to quote one student. According to another student, they "observe Negroes through their little microscope of manipulation. . . ."

At the same time, no White wanted to discuss even the possibility of anything related to mistrust; to speak of it made its existence more real. Again, the difficulty was increased by the prospect of a formal investigation. A White activist noted that "Once [Whites] admitted a prejudice [towards themselves by the Negro] they had to leave." When she saw a pen and paper appear, the comment was rephrased and tempered so that "a prejudice" gave way to "communication between the races is hard." When she saw the comment recorded, it was rephrased and tempered again; this time "hard" was replaced with "not easy." Or the respondents went beyond disavowing their answers, they disavowed the question. In order to protect what they preferred to consider their racial anonymity, efforts were made to repudiate the question. The attempted repudiation meant lowering the position of the interviewer ("It seems like you want to bring up all the dirt"); or elevating their own position (the reply to "How do you cope with being a White in [a predominantly Negro civil rights organization]?" was "You might better ask: 'How do I cope with being a White in a racist society?'").

However, a more informal approach that avoided

references to a study did not eliminate the defenses; instead, it brought out their complexity. Whatever recognition Whites have of their situation is usually enveloped by several layers that are, moving towards the outside, ascendingly palatable. The only White student attending a Negro college was encountered at a conference sponsored by a civil rights organization; because the relevance of race was part of the formal proceedings, it was comparatively easy to take it as a point of departure for conversation with him. He was asked whether there was anything he did or did not do at school because he was White. He indicated there was nothing. As a means of returning to this question, further along, he was asked whether he dated students. He then explained that he avoided dating, because "I don't like to dance." In other words, the explanation could be found within himself, and it was totally unrelated to race. After additional conversation and questioning, his case against dating was that when they went into town "it would be dangerous for the girl." Here race is acknowledged as a factor, but only so far as the segregationist White introduces it. Later in the conversation, the subject was reintroduced amidst considerable probing. He eventually indicated that dating would be opposed by the students. His elaboration suggested that he had appraised the situation in detail. He explained that the preceding year a White girl at the college dated Negro students, "but that is different." In view of traditional relationships in the South, he saw dating a Negro girl as leading to objections that would be "instinctual" (the term suggests there is still a protective covering: the resistance he cites is a survival; therefore, it is removed from reasoning and himself).

Regardless of these obstacles, the fact remains that the nature of trust appears most clearly when its absence can be examined. But there is rarely an opportunity, as here, to examine a widely encompassing and sustained contact that is permeated by mistrust. At almost every point where the relationship is incomplete, the reason can be traced to some missing aspect of trust that is ordinarily taken for granted when it is obscured by its presence.

However, the absence of trust is often obscured as well. Although jealousy is a state of mistrust, one half of a "couple" can be jealous of the other half without causing a rupture in the relationship, for jealousy is popularly defined as a proof of devotion. But contacts within the Movement lack the tradition necessary to develop a rhetoric that perpetually obscures mistrust. They further lack the necessary mutual interest (for that of one party is not sufficient) to formulate such a rhetoric.

By trust, an act of faith is not implied here; instead, it is assumed that trust results from calculations, whether or not conscious, such as those that appear in the following effort at an operational definition of the term. These calculations are intended to control the extent to which A and B can disadvantage each other. Further, trust cannot occur unless the risks already appear to have been eliminated within the foreseeable limits of the prospective relationship. The break between the appraisal preceding trust and trust itself is complete; the act of trust is free of all the calculations that characterized its prelude, since they have served their purpose. As a result, the phrase "implicit trust" is redundant. For trust is achieved when A feels his control over B is sufficient to assure that B will act with A absent the same way he would with A present. More specific requirements of trust include:

Continuity. The claims made by B concerning his part in the prospective relationship correspond with the experience of A.

Indivisibility. Trust cannot be fragmented; in order to achieve a trust relationship in one sphere of activity with B, A cannot have violated the trust of B in any other sphere.

Commonality. A determines that not only would he be better off in the prospective trust relationship than by acting alone, but that B has an equivalent need for this reliance.

Scrutability. A believes he knows, and is in agreement with, the reasons behind the stated intent of B.

Invulnerability. A considers that B has too much to lose or, at least, nothing to gain by acting contrary to his stated purpose.

Durability. A is able to assume that B will not change (for the worse) once trust has been conferred.

Plausibility. The prospective reward of A cannot appear disproportionately greater than that of B; otherwise, the asymmetry will be "too good to be true."

Insularity. When A is satisfied that in case of competing claims between himself and C who endangers him, B will choose A.

These prerequisites operate regardless of race, but they appear to Negroes appraising Whites with greater force. This relevance can be seen in a detailed case of insularity. Before A is willing to provide B with guilty knowledge, he must be convinced that B is a terminal point in their communication network, so that the information will not be passed on to the endangering C. If A is a Negro, and B as well as C are Whites, concern with C multiplies; since they are Whites, B and C are more likely to be considered as part of a collectivity, not as distinct individuals. In broad terms, there is no basis for effectively bartering trust with Whites.

C. J. L.

CONTENTS

Preface

one
CONTENTMENT   1

Remoteness of the White Protects Him from Mistrust
Proximity of the White Protects Him from Mistrust
Remoteness of the Negro Protects the White from Mistrust

two
INDIGNATION   21

three
AWKWARDNESS   29

Mechanics of Exemption-seeking
Laboratory of Exemption-seeking
Collapse of Exemption-seeking

four
DISMAY   69

Vulnerability of Conversion-claimants
Whites Assisted by Negroes Obstruct the Conversion
Negroes Assisted by Whites Obstruct the Conversion
A Successful Conversion by Whites that Is Self-defeating
Negroes Are Freed from Their Attempted Conversion
Whites Are Freed from Their Attempted Conversion

chapter one

CONTENTMENT

The White seeking to assist Southern Negroes has provided himself with a variety of shields against their mistrust; the type of shield varying with the nature and degree of his distance from the Negroes. When the distance is geographic and extended, no shield has been necessary, or more accurately, this form of distance acts as a shield. The fund-raising material for a Southern Negro college is prepared by a public relations firm in New York City and declares that its client "is a powerful factor in the creation of better race relations"; meantime, the Northern White donors of the College are accused by the student government president, in a speech to students, of "Perpetuating indignities and oppression on the students."

As the mistrust in civil rights organizations developed from nuances to headlines, distance ceased to be a shield for their White donors in the North. The following section is, therefore, one of those that is recording history. Nevertheless, since it was studied as an on-going activity, the present tense is used.

The narrow contact that the donor has with the Southern-based civil rights organizations limits the amount of mistrust he is exposed to, but not the amount he activates. Both the cause and effect of having to shield him from mistrust result in its magnification. Shielding is necessary because the donations are necessary. Yet, the reliance on donations means the Negro must revert to a traditional relationship with the White. The implications of this reliance are not bound by the limited contact: "We have to castrate ourselves every day for pennies." The extent to which financial dependency means a reversion is suggested in the following account that was written by a Negro civil rights worker and posted on the door of his office after he returned South:

> As a slave or serf, I went to the landowner [Whites in a Northern office of the organization] and asked for money to return to the plantation [the national office], and the landowners used lies, deceit, and all to deny me the money to get back to the plantation. I contend now that if there had been no landowners, then we slaves would have no trouble trying to travel back to the plantation. Our slave headquarters in [the North] must be run as other headquarters throughout slave land, it must be run and controlled by slaves.
>
> An embittered slave
> who wants to control

When alternatives to the donations from Whites are considered, they usually make the dependence still clearer. A Negro who was organizing in a rural area complained about "Negroes going North, saying 'I'm hungry.' I'm sick of that. They give them a box of food and a box of clothes and satisfy their guilt." He therefore proposed that a "freedom herd" be started in the county where he was working, but this raised the problem of where enough money was available to purchase the cows.

The White in the North is encouraged to believe that he is already trusted. Instructions for Northern fund raisers included the suggestion that "intimate details of what goes on in the field" and additional devices be used to "make them [prospective donors] feel on the inside." Although he had little hope for its success, a Negro staff member considered, in a report, fund raising in Northern Negro ghettos since their inhabitants were authentically on the inside:

> This type of fund-raising may help to relieve some of the guilt feelings that [Negroes in the South soliciting Northern funds] are experiencing. The picture of sup-

pression is more relevant to people with similar problems, which means that you don't have to look for ghastly stories to tell in order to get money.

Donations are invited and rewarded by means of form letters from the South suggesting that this help is sufficient to prove that the contributor, in turn, trusts the Negro: "We need the continued support of all people of good will. . . . Contributions are more than money—they are affirmations of confidence in and dedication to democratic change."

At about the same time this letter was composed, its author noted that alliances with Whites were all right in their place, but he delimited this place by a reference to the "white elements" whose presence means "no militant movement can afford to relax its vigilance against half-hearted associates or conscious betrayers." However, the statement was for internal consumption; the only Whites who heard it were staff members.

Transient engagement provides another shield from mistrust. The White whose involvement is limited by time, is as well protected as the one who is limited by space. The Selma to Montgomery march provided an opportunity for a short-term witness. Most of those attracted had come South for the last phase of the march; in many cases the Whites arrived and departed on the same day. Further, participants were surrounded by other transients, often other delegates from the same group. The consequent restrictions on their exposure formed an effective shield from mistrust.

A comparison of the narratives written by two marchers, Negro and White, suggests they were in the same event and different worlds. The following aspects of Whites have been drawn from the account written by the White:[1]

[1] Maurice N. Eisendrath, "President's Perspective," *American Judaism* (Summer, 1965), p. 3.

1. *Ennobled.* "For the Montgomery demonstration was a religiously inspired, morally motivated, divinely impassioned declaration by white and Negroes, clergy and laymen, men, women, and children from all parts of the nation that they chose liberty—or death."
2. *Sacrificial.* ". . . that most deeply religious experience which found me rising at four in the morning and marching with tens of thousands of Negroes, many fellow Jews, rabbis and laymen, but altogether not nearly enough whites. We walked through the sleazy slums of Montgomery, greeted en route by hostile eyes and an occasional coarse invective."
3. *Emancipating.* "A modern Jericho, it will be known to future generations of Americans as the place where the walls of special privilige began to tumble as trumpets of social responsibility sounded the summons to 'overcome.' "
4. *Oppressed.* "Montgomery, Alabama, will indeed live in the history of our country, along with Valley Forge and Gettysburg, as a place where the will to be free hardened into an invincible determination for thousands of diverse individuals with the odds against them."

While the account by the Negro suggests the Whites were:[2]

1. *Hypocritical.* "As the White Northerners poured into the city, for the first time in their lives many of them slept in Negro homes, prayed in Negro churches, and stood beside a Negro with a feeling of equanimity. They had all run from the North to condemn the South for slavery and serfdom but few of them ever faced the problem in their own backyard."
2. *Insensitive.* "The Whites marching next to Cager

[2] William Mahoney, "The March to Montgomery," *Présence Africaine* (Third Quarter, 1965), pp. 183–184.

Lee would never understand how totally Cager Lee's enemy is violence, the violence of a society built upon slavery."

3. *Deserting*. ". . . the businessmen who will leave the South on the next train."

4. *Dominating*. "With the arrival of the influential Northern Whites, the control of the movement passed from the hands of indigenous Negroes."

PROXIMITY OF THE WHITE PROTECTS HIM FROM MISTRUST

The White who is involved with the cause of Southern Negroes close at hand for an extended period is, for the time being, equally well protected from mistrust. What he regards as a psychological proximity to Negroes is an effective shield. Vis-à-vis himself, the White is "passing" as a Negro. His submergence in what he considers to be Blackness provides its own shelter. One White civil rights worker described part of her brief return North in a memoir:

> I went to a meeting of the Ethical Culture one Sunday after I came home from _____, and do you know what we did? We came in our high heels, and sat in chairs placed in neat rows facing a pulpit in the front of the room. First a lady got up and read a quotation about Thoughts for the New Year. Then another lady played a piece by Shumann on the piano, and then we all got up and sang four neat little verses. When we sat down again, the leader, _____, spoke to us from the pulpit about four qualities we should think about developing for the New Year—something like foresight, charity, dedication, and love. Then the lady at the piano played another polite little piece, and then it was all over. I could have cried in frustration. Do you know what I wanted to do? I would have made them pull the chairs around into a circle, and

> had husbands and wives put their arms around each
> other, and had the children sit in their parents' laps,
> and then I would have started them clapping and sing-
> ing—something in parts. And I wouldn't have been
> satisfied until I'd gotten them feeling each other, and
> themselves, creating. That's what you should do at a
> Sunday meeting—that's how you worship God.

In effect, there has been no departure from the South, since
the religious form of the Negro, or her view of it, is superim-
posed on what had once been her own.

In almost every sector of his thinking and activity the
White has a need to feel as one with the Negro, so that he
becomes gratefully dependent on the Negro. However, the
dependency of the Negro on the White in the Movement is
highly limited and grudging. The resultant disparity gives
the White an investment in trusting the Negro which is not
reciprocated. The investment, in turn, causes the White to
lower his criteria for trust from where they would operate in
a situation of mutual dependence. In other words, the need
of the White to have his trust reciprocated helps account for
his inability to see that it has not been.

The dependence of the White largely results from a
rejection of the White world and, in its place, an acceptance
of the Negro world. The two factors are closely related. The
rejection is used by the White as a basis for acceptance; he
offers it to the Negro and himself as certification of his disengagement from Whiteness.

But as the civil rights movement shifted from a lost
to a won cause (the transition occurred around 1964, and co-
incided with, among other activities, the Civil Rights Law),
participation in it acquired a greater continuity with the
White world. In turn, the White recruits have been increasingly less marginal. A White who joined the Movement before the transition notes that it was then considered "exotic"
and accordingly attracted "the best—and the worst . . . now

going to the South is respectable," so that it attracts "a middle-range type of person: the Joe College type." It has become possible for Whites to journey South without severing their ties to the campus—which is the source of most recruits. Programs initiated by organizations in the North have made the South an extension of the Northern campus: one-year teaching appointments at Negro colleges that will not interfere with the completion of a doctorate are arranged; students can become activists in the Delta for the duration of their Thanksgiving vacation. As a result of this continuity, participants in the Movement are less alienated than formerly when, for instance, students who left Northern campuses were less likely to return, whether or not they remained as civil rights workers. They were willing to remain in jail for several months rather than pay bail; it later became common to pay this bail instead of serving out the sentence.

The earlier participants were often the last remains of the so-called Beat Generation. The Negro had served the Beats as a natural resource; much of their culture had been derived from him. He was no less the archetype of jazz than he was of "being on the road"—from Africa to the South, and through migrations North.

Although these earlier participants were objectively more alienated in terms of the discontinuity from their origins, the later ones were more likely to believe themselves alienated. Alienation is "in." The term has become commonly used for self-description as well as a focus for marginal journals that are subscribed to and "radical" political organizations that are joined; all of which means that alienation now provides a sense of belonging.

A seamless bond with the Negro, expressed through a trust relationship, still appears to the White as the most convincing proof of alienation. At the same time, the Negro offers the only discernible means to the ersatz community that is needed by the White. Although the objective dependency on the Negro in this respect may be less than before, the subjective dependency is, if anything, greater, for the value of the Negro has been enhanced. Blackness, too, is *de rigueur*. A White civil rights worker notes, "A lot of people are in the Movement because they're alienated from White society, and Black is what's happening, and they want to identify with Black. The White community is what they're running away from—there's no sex appeal." In fact, Blackness is so much in style that it is being imported for those who are not physically "running away." A shop in New York advertises its "Soul Clothing" (that the term has also run away from its origins is indicated by its including Batman shirts and John Pershing jackets).

Partly through popularization and commercialization, Blackness serves as a symbol of the noble savage. In turn, the noble savage serves as a shelter from all that is popularized and commercialized, with what is regarded as the accompanying stultification. A White in the Movement notes that Negroes have "the healthiest life in the world," whereas "White minds are always cracking up; the hospitals are full of them. You can't get along very long without love—without your body, Freud says." A White who was once deeply involved in the Movement, continues to see the world in terms of: "White is rigidity; Negro is freedom." This typical concept persists even though it has very often been Whites who promote freedom, while Negroes promote rigidity (these Whites were said, by these Negroes, to be "freedom high"). An example of the disparity appeared during a staff meeting when a White argued in favor of a worker traveling from project to project, because "It would be his way of expressing himself." One of the Negroes commented: "This isn't a psychiatric clinic. If you want to express yourself, you can take up painting."

The romanticism that formulates the nobility of the savage is closely connected with another source of the White dependency. As stated by an officer of a predominantly White civil rights organization, its members are "absolving guilt." The Negro alone can grant absolution, which provides him with the most penetrating form of dominance. It is so penetrating that the romanticization appears to be, in part, an attempt at assisting the absolution by providing an assurance that the Negro has transcended his mistreatment and turned it on its head. The White thereby reduces the grounds for his guilt. The capacity of the White for such romanticism appeared when a new faculty member at a Negro college heard a campaign speech there by a White soliciting Negro votes. To dramatize Negro oppression, the candidate noted that Negro children were forced to play amid "rusty old cars." The White instructor considered this "a great idea." He decided that his son would enjoy a rusty old car, and set about obtaining one for their backyard (though he abandoned the plan when reminded what his middle class Negro neighbors would think).

Although romanticized, and to the extent he is, the Negro gives the White access to what is viewed as the political reality, and, moreover, the expectation of triumphing in it. Accordingly, a White teacher prepared a guidebook for the student civil rights organization on campus; its recommendations included the following:

> With the help of Air Force ROTC members and enough contributions to get one 4 (or 6) seater plane and one helicopter, you can set up a ——— AIR FORCE ("Freedom Airways") for instant transportation *and other operations* (see me about this).

One of the proposed "other operations" was landing a helicopter in front of the Selma, Alabama, court house in order to make a citizen's arrest of Sheriff James Clark, and then flying off with him. The Negro becomes the retriever of forlorn hopes. He is invested with a power to accomplish what the White has dreamed and despaired of accomplishing. One White civil rights worker described Negroes as "the only group in the country that can change it fundamentally"; for the middle class White, Negroes fill the vacuum left by disenchantment with the working class.

REMOTENESS OF THE NEGRO PROTECTS THE WHITE FROM MISTRUST

The other side of this psychological proximity, as the White considers it, is a psychological remoteness from the Negro that also acts as a shield. This remoteness facilitates his misinterpretation of mistrust signals; for all practical purposes, they initially fail to reach him just as though he were geographically removed.

To some extent, the failure results from the form in which these signals are transmitted by the Negro living in a rural Southern community. He reacts to the White civil rights worker in much the same way he has always reacted to Whites, and the reaction is disguised in the traditional manner. In short, mistrust becomes ingratiation. A resident of one such community described how his fellow Negroes handle mistrust: "They go out of their way to hide it." Deference is a shield provided by the Negro, since it results in mistrust being mistaken for trust. But as a Negro civil rights worker explained about the behavior of the local Negro toward the White activist: "If he treats you better than he treats himself —forget it. That's not respect, and that's not trust. He's doing it because he thinks that's what the White man wants him to do." The civil rights workers have no reason for verifying the apparent trust. A veteran White activist states that "people like it—they were treated like White heroes." The generous welcome corresponds with their own pictures of themselves.

Their remoteness from the Negro community also

means that if the Whites should seek verification, they would have difficulty in finding it. The main problem is lack of an undeniable base line. Initially, the Whites have little knowledge of how the Negro acts when they are not present. However, the preferential treatment received by Whites frequently contrasts Negro behavior with them present and absent. But where this happens, as in one case at dinner when the White guests were treated on a much grander scale than the Negroes were treating themselves, it does not register. Rather than determine how the other Whites interpreted the deference, it went unacknowledged: "We never talked about it." The reluctance to seek verification meant these Whites avoided another base line they had access to—each other.

Nevertheless, sufficient exposure to the Negro community leads to a mistrust verification being thrust upon the White civil rights worker. In the case of the indulged diners, mistrust was first recognized about a year after they initiated their voter registration project. When they failed at recruiting local Negroes to help with the work: "Suddenly it hit us." The significance of their Whiteness to the local Negroes had finally begun to emerge. As stated by one of the Whites, "In looking back, I can see things. When we came in people were open to us; but it was because we were White, not because of what we stood for." The shock of recognition was all the greater for being retroactive.

Verification was made still more vivid by the Whites gaining partial access to the formerly concealed realm of Negro thought. To the extent Whites appeared to gain acceptance, they learned of their unacceptance. The reason for the recruitment failure was articulated by a local Negro whom one of the Whites "got to know real well." He explained that the White organizers "could go back to their jobs or go back to college."

The exposure to undisguised mistrust does not mean the White is automatically able to feel its depth. The last quote, for instance, says far more about mistrust than the White is usually willing or able to concede after limited involvement in the Negro community. For it suggests that the White civil rights worker and the Negro stand in a totally different relation to the undertaking which is supposed to demonstrate their unity. The White has a recourse unavailable to the Negro. As a result, there is no check operating on the White to assure that his acts will benefit the Negro. The general feeling of his community, as stated by a Negro, was that in the event Whites engaged there in civil rights activity "can do something beneficial," there would still be a fear that they "can always mess up." No matter what he does, the White supposedly has nothing to lose through his activity in the Negro community. While the Negro, who is comparatively stationary, has everything to lose.

In short, there is nothing to offset the traditional mistrust of the White. The Negro does not have enough leverage to keep the relationship from being entirely subject to the discretion of the White (therefore, the prospect of withdrawal has the same source, and menaces to the same extent, as the reverse one that the White will get overly involved in the Movement so that he dominates it). A Negro in another community said that when White, as opposed to Negro, civil rights workers arrive, the local Negroes "look more deeply into it." Accordingly, they ask " 'Why are [the Whites] here? They don't have to be here.' " Further, it is assumed that because " 'he doesn't have to be here, his interest is superficial. He's here to have a good time; because all his friends are coming down and he doesn't want to be a square.' " One Negro speculated on what would happen to the communities when "something else becomes hip and everyone [White] leaves."

However, the White sees his stay as a permanent one, for the Movement is his universe; it sets his psychic clock.

When asked how long he plans to stay, the typical answer is "indefinitely." Precisely because thoughts about the transience of his stay would lead him to the same conclusion that the Negro has come to, he cannot afford them. His situation is governed by a tautology: he regards himself as a permanent resident (of the Movement, if not the specific community), since he is totally committed; since he regards himself as totally committed, he is a permanent resident.

The capacity of the White to sense mistrust partly depends on how much the circumstances of that community cause him to feel he loses by remaining there. His sense of mistrust is inversely related to his sense of loss. For instance, early in the Movement, when violence was relatively prevalent, the conflict between civil rights organizations and segregationists made the internal conflict between Negroes and Whites less evident to the White. Violence allowed the White to focus on his sacrifice, and he assumed the Negro did as well. One of these early White participants regarded beatings as a way to "prove yourself . . . that was all there was to it; you were one of the boys, not one of the White boys."

But this is not necessarily the way the Negroes saw it. When Negro civil rights workers are in the company of Movement Whites, they are all unmistakable targets. According to one of these Negroes, "I'm more likely to get shot . . . it increases my visibility." Concomitantly, the visibility of the Movement White, as seen by the Negro, is increased. A White was asked, by Negroes riding in the car with her, to conceal herself while passing Mississippi State Patrolmen who were looking for them. She refused. In effect, she refused to acknowledge that she was different from her fellow passengers. The roadblock had made them particularly aware of what one referred to as her "flaming red hair." But her refusal underscored another dimension of Whiteness—

her inability to feel "a sense of the reality of the danger." Where Whites are more responsive, the problem is not solved. An early Negro participant observed that he and a White had "learned to fight together, but we didn't learn to live together." In looking back, even the harmony of their fighting together seems incomplete: "It's a common cause, but it's more common for me than it is for him."

Also relevant to the rate of discovery is the willingness of a community to reveal its mistrust, which depends on how much its members feel they have to lose in the process. An increasing number of Negroes in civil rights organizations have felt there is nothing to be lost. At worst, White support will be lost, but they also feel this would be best in any case. A Negro in one organization that was heavily dependent on White skills and funds said about the prospect of losing them: "I don't care if it sets us back ten years." Those who feel similarly do not hesitate to let the White participants know "if I had my way, I'd get rid of all the White people in ———."

Whereas, the vulnerability of the rural Negro to economic and other reprisals combines with the indistinguishability of Whites to produce a reserve. At the opposite economic extreme, a reserve results from another form of vulnerability. The comparatively prosperous Negro is often concerned with the preservation of a private world that spares him the realities of race. Indulging his feelings toward Whites would not allow him to remain a racial neuter. Since the White teachers are in the midst of an otherwise sheltered community and must be contended with, a *modus vivendi* is found through the instrument of formality.

Formality is a pantomime of trust. At times it has the appearance, but never the feeling, of trust. Formality is initiated by the Negro faculty as a way of building relationships on a base of mistrust. If it does not make mistrust felicitous, it at least keeps it unacknowledged, and thereby postpones, for both White and Negro, the necessity of having to come to terms with it.

It is easier for the Negro than the White to sustain formality. First of all, the Negro is more accustomed to it. The arm's length arrangement with White faculty is only a variation of the traditional relationship with Whites. In addition, the terms of the formality are established by the Negro. These are the terms for "correct" behavior, which usually appear incorrect to the White.

On the other hand, formality has a short-term advantage for the White. It limits the possibility of racial indiscretions. Formality comprises the only systematic rules for behavior offered by Negroes to the White. It is reassuring for the White to have this sort of road map—except when he realizes the destination of the route he is following is in the opposite direction from trust.

The guidelines establish the precise terms for "friendliness." The narrow definition for this relationship was communicated to a White faculty member and his wife who gave a party for all members of his department and their wives. The wife notes that although no one attended, the "people [invited] are friendly" when later encountered casually or professionally. Since then, the same couple has had two receptions for new or visiting faculty. All members of the department attended these without their wives; it was, she says "a business relationship." The rules implied here are those usually applied, in other contexts, to relations with Negroes by Whites.

Initially, Whites suppose the Negro faculty are simply being friendly. Later, it is described as "Everybody's friendly —in a detached way." A final perspective was at work when a White instructor, who had helped organize a civil rights conference on campus, afterward encountered a conservative Negro faculty member who remarked: "That certainly was an interesting conference you had." "But," added the White to his description of the encounter, "under their breaths they're saying 'You miserable sonofabitch.' " The friendliness is seen as an act of aggression.

If the White pointedly disregards the guidelines of formality, and confronts the Negro with it, the outcome can easily demonstrate how effectively the Negro had been previously restrained. One Negro instructor abided by the rules of formality so carefully that a White instructor noted that "you have to interpret what he says." Once when this Negro was being evasive, another White faculty member probed to get fuller information. According to the White, the Negro suddenly began "yelling and hollering that I was impugning his motives."

In their contacts with Whites, formality imposes a restraint on Negroes that is absent from their relations with Negroes (except when Whites are present). A Negro instructor observed, "Negroes invite their White friends to gatherings, but it's only when the Negroes go off by themselves that they enjoy themselves." The other side of this informality was demonstrated by an administrator at a Negro college who never hesitated to show displeasure, often violently, when provoked by Negro faculty members; but toward equally provoking White faculty members, he acted, when most hostile, in a manner that was described by one of them as no more than "imperious." The suspension of formality also permits undisguised antagonism.

Yet, this antagonism is considered by Negroes to be of a different nature when directed against other Negroes. The difference was made clear in a civil rights organization, where formality also operated—though more informally. One of the females in the office was White, and she was, according to the female Negro workers, "very unwelcome," a fact that they tried to communicate by acting "real cold" toward her: "We don't even want to talk to her." At the same time, they did not hesitate to use profanities toward each other, because "We understand each other . . . we won't take it for harm." To a considerable extent, intraracial antagonism meets with a greater resiliency because of the greater access to conviviality.

Race is at the bottom of formality in two senses. Besides being largely responsible for its development, race is deep enough within formality to never, in the normal course of affairs, make a public appearance. Much of formality is devoted to establishing ways of simultaneously making race the principal criterion and keeping it unacknowledged. At a nominating committee meeting, a White instructor was being considered for president of an organization when the one Negro on the committee argued against him by telling the other two teachers, both White, that "We need a balance between the older and newer faculty members." Her White colleagues were ready for the next stage, since they understood "newer" to be a euphemism.

chapter two

INDIGNATION

The second stage is characterized by a partial recognition of the mistrust, and a total rejection of its legitimacy. Because he does not sense the depth of this mistrust, the grounds presented for it appear, at best, irrelevant. No attempt is made, nor need felt, to deal with it on the same terms that produced it. The response is framed in terms that helped produce, and therefore confirm, the mistrust. So far from offering a defense, the White indicates that only he knows when the Negro is entitled to be mistrustful.

This is not to say the White at this stage is unconcerned, but his concern is more with the Negro who makes the charge, than with the charge itself. A civil rights organization spokesman had said in a speech: "I don't know why White people get involved in the Movement." In response, a White person wrote its headquarters: "That's a ridiculous statement for a _____ leader to make. I'm White, and I can tell him why I got involved." Moreover, he wanted the spokesman condemned for a statement that was "ridiculous."

"Ridiculous" is a caricature of indignation; it exaggerates the two opposing qualities of this condition. There is an element of disturbance to indignation that arises from one person considering another to have not met his obligations. But there is a concurrent element of assurance, since it is also believed that measures are at hand for correcting the other's offense.

This second element means that indignation is not so much a loss of control as an assertion of it. When it was known that many Negroes did not want a forthcoming civil rights activity to be desegregated, a White woman who had

23

been on the periphery of the Movement explained in her application for the event that she wanted to "demonstrate for inclusion of 'whites.' I don't approve of 'exclusion' whether white or black." A recently arrived White teacher, who questioned one of his students about problems in the classroom, was told that "many students consider the White man and Negro irreconcilable." The teacher replied that this outlook was "inappropriate between individuals." Another White instructor expressed his sense of disapproval and inappropriateness, that is, of indignation, in a less tempered form. After a student provided him with his first information about mistrust toward White faculty, the instructor told a third party: "I was talking to him like a man—and he was talking to me like a White man. I'm going to hit that sonofabitch in his goddamned puss."

The restricted vision of the White at this point is largely due to the value he puts on his services, a value that provides the assurance necessary for indignation. It is inconceivable to him, but assumed by the Negro, that although working for the Movement, he might not be benefiting it. As suggested by the following cases from disparate settings, the belief of the White that he is making a contribution is sufficient to overcome any charges by the Negro to the contrary, including charges based on mistrust.

A White faculty member at a Negro college sent an appeal for used books to the student body of a Midwestern university. In emphasizing the needs of the local students, he mentioned the school was "in the middle of nowhere." As a result, according to his wife, "You've never seen such racial furor." The grievances were never presented directly, but they learned that this phrase was considered patronizing by the administration of their college. After reflecting on the episode, she concludes: "I suppose asking ——— students to donate books to ——— students was condescending. But whom do you care about: the image of the administrator, or the benefit of the student?"

Two Northerners, a White and a Negro, were working on the election campaign of Negro candidates in a Southern community. An elderly Negro man offered to help on election day, but added that he would like to vote early. The White, who will be called Mark, gave him an assignment that would have prevented an early vote. When the Negro activist protested, the White pointed out, "He'll do anything we ask." In his account of the exchange, the Negro activist suggested a more complete statement would have been "He'll do anything we, Mark, ask him." He therefore wanted the old Negro to make his own decision. Mark presented his side of the incident by conceding the old Negro "would have done it because I was White . . . [but by voting early] he'd have to wait in line from eight to nine-thirty, which I consider prime time; I saw it in the larger perspective."

Although the protesting Negroes cannot be by-passed so easily when they are also the recipients of these efforts, the indignation of the White is still apparent (however, the eventual coming-to-terms with this protest is brought closer, since he is thwarted more directly). The following was sent to the Southern headquarters of a civil rights organization by a White working in one of its Northern offices:

> For a ——— office in the North to work well, there must be a certain type of relation or understanding between National ——— in [the South] and the office in the North. There must be some type of coordination from some point. To carry on fund raising activities in the North there must be some type of response to our desperate cries for help. ——— is growing everyday and we must be able to keep in touch with the growth of ———. Groups working in the North should or must have a more active participation within ———.

Groups in the North must be able to state their position about certain matters (affecting them and maybe
National ——) without being set upon by someone
in the [national] office. We all have to give and take.
Give and take in the sense that there is cooperation,
and cooperation from both ends of the field. Phone
calls MUST be returned, and returned not four or five
days later. We should be in on the decision making
(that which affects the North). Aware of the fact that
—— is the National Office and that there are certain
lines along which —— works but —— must also
become aware that there are certain problems that
exist in the North and by being South one isn't always
familiar with these problems. Not only should the
Northern Staff take a more active participation in the
activities of ——, but those working with us (The
chairman of the local —— or ——). Please don't
misunderstand me, I'm not saying that every Tom,
Dick and Harry as well as Mary and Sallie Sue should
take or be in such a position, but those whom we know
are workers, those who have worked with —— since
it's beginning and those whom we know are committed to the principles and goals of ——. These people should and must have a role within ——, a role
that is more than that of some one up North (a do-
gooder) who is trying to clear his or her conscience
for some strange reason.

The symptoms of mistrust are visible to the White; he is
excluded from decision making and "set upon" for trying to
become part of it. But he counters with what the Negroes in
the national office "must" do. The more explicit form of mistrust, in which his motives are discredited, is dealt with by
another imperative.

The Negroes as well as Whites would agree that books
and voter registration and efficiency are good. The only point
of disagreement is on the weight given to Whiteness. The

Whites take everything into account except Whiteness. The Negroes take little into account except Whiteness; those in the national office would define efficiency as something more than the result of a time-and-motion study. One Negro activist wrote a paper entitled "Racial Considerations Among the Staff," in which he conceded an area of utility provided by Whites, but felt it was offset by related areas of their participation:

> It is apparent that whites bring wider publicity and thus wider support. Yet, it is also apparent that integrated groups in segregated areas are "spotlights" and that certain groupings, i.e., white women and black men, are a "declaration of war." It is also true, I feel that there is a sort of "ethnic relationship" among the staff and community; I do not feel that this relationship can be entered into by Whites.

To the Negro, the presence of Whites in the Movement is inefficient.

The brevity of this chapter reflects the brevity of this stage, for the balance between disturbance and assurance is a delicate one. Indignation is not self-contained; there is no way for it to continue operating once the basis for its assurance is seen to be nonexistent: students did not read the imported books, and Mark had little success recruiting Negro voters. The "larger perspective" that he referred to begins to appear smaller than the one used by the Negro.

chapter three

AWKWARDNESS

The mistrust of the Negro is real to the White at this stage. He has no doubts about its depth. But he cannot yet accept its scope. He still considers himself trustworthy; he therefore rejects any mistrust directed against him. This stage is principally devoted to protecting the exemption he feels is rightfully his.

Efforts to achieve exemption are undertaken in a setting that one White teacher described as "awkward, very awkward." The awkwardness that characterizes this stage has several bases. One is the enormity of the loss should the exemption not be conferred. The failure would be irreversible. For the supposed immunity to mistrust would be lost, and the White already knows, as did one teacher from watching the response of Negroes to other Whites, that where this happens, "It would all come out." Another teacher considered his experiences to resemble "walking on eggs"; this image reflects the fact that every step he takes involves the likelihood of destroying his only foundation.

MECHANICS OF EXEMPTION-SEEKING

The awkwardness is magnified by the unavailability of an established program for achieving exemption. The guidelines developed by individual participants provide little guidance. For instance, "You bend, sometimes you let yourself be broken; you take your stand, and let the chips fall where they may." These bromides indicate a distance from the realm of experience. At the same time, contradiction within them describes the bafflement of the White. His guideline is not so much a means of imposing order on his context, as a reflection of the disorder he finds in it.

In describing his efforts to secure the trust of his class-mates, particularly those active in civil rights, at a Negro college, a White noted that "You think you're qualified, but you don't know what he [the Negro] thinks is qualified." It becomes clear that some kind of guideline is necessary since acting "naturally" has what the White considers an unnatural effect on the Negro. A Negro civil rights worker asked a White volunteer if he knew that "very few Africans wear glasses." The White replied: "That's because most Africans can't read." Another Negro objected because "I take that very personally." The White said to her, "I was just telling the truth; do you want me to lie?" She answered, "No." In re-calling this exchange, the White asked himself aloud: "What am I supposed to do?"

The divergence between the effect that the White wants to have on the Negro and the effect he does have is a consequence of not yet knowing the extent to which he is seen as White. A White teacher who expected to be more closely involved in the campus community by serving on a library committee, instead found himself further removed from it. He had proposed an innovation, and upon hearing it was already under consideration, commented: "I didn't know you knew about that." The Negro librarian later noted how much the Negroes on his staff had "resented" this statement. As he saw it, the problem was that "people mistake his tact-lessness for racial arrogance."

Instead of providing grounds for exemption from Whiteness, the techniques used by the Whites are more likely to provide the Negro with grounds for exempting them from the Movement. At the staff meeting of a civil rights organiza-tion, a Negro stated:

> All my life I've been dominated. Whites try to take over everything. One time I tried to say that wasn't true. But it happened in Mississippi in 1964, when all those White kids came and took over, because we sat

around discussing what a problem they are and what are we going to do about it. As many can come down as want to [now], but we're just going to outwork them.

While Negroes thought to "outwork" Whites was a solution, Whites thought outworking the Negro would solve their problem. But the White did not succeed in having it viewed as dedication; instead, their sedulousness often provided Negroes with proof the Whites were trying to "take over" the organization. In addition, the work of Whites was capable of derailing the program of Negroes. A White working in one county continued driving local people to the voting registrar after the Negro civil rights workers decided these prospective voters needed the sense of independence that would come from providing their own transportation.

The White assumes he controls the effect of his Whiteness. This assumption is itself an extension of Whiteness. More specifically, the White is suggesting that he only alerts the Negro to his Whiteness when he makes references to race or color that are both artless and explicit. It means, essentially, he is only White when he says he is, and when he says he is, it is by accident: a lack of control. After two Negro colleagues asked about his apartment, a White instructor said, "It's black and dreary," and thought, "Oh boy, I'm in the soup again." The remoteness of a metaphor, such as this, that is considered to trigger racial awareness for the Negro, is not yet considered to be a cue that there are no clear delimitations to this awareness.

For the White has yet to recognize it is generally not these signals that alert the Negro to Whiteness, but that the Whiteness alerts the Negro to the signals. As one Negro teacher said about others vis-à-vis the White teacher: "They're always waiting for him to make a slip." Or, as another Negro put it after a White had incriminated himself: "That was what they wanted to believe." Because of this need to confirm their mistrust, the evidence needed for confirmation may be generated by the mistrust.

The primacy given to Whiteness means that all contingencies are covered, including those that may be opposite from each other. A student, who insisted the teacher had given low grades "because he's White," concluded, "Mr. ——— hung me out on the last test, but he won't do it this time. No White man will mess over me like that." A second student referred to what happened after her classmates complained that the same examination had been unduly difficult: "That man shouldn't have apologized for the test. He did it just because he's White, and scared down here." The inflexibility of mistrust in its refusal to consider trust possibilities provides an extreme flexibility when it comes to the choice of acts or words for substantiating mistrust.

It follows that the White is also unable to control the signals. His usual effort is toward emitting signals that will call attention to not being White. While a group of White instructors demonstrated against what they claimed was the autocratic administration of their college, students told each other, as related by one: "Now you've got a Black President; it's what you've been fighting for: Black supremacy. Look at the people who are pushing—they're all White." The Whites had managed, as a student noted, to "bring in the race issue"; this had been their objective, but they were placed on the wrong side of the issue. The Whites had hoped they would be seen in terms of the cause; this too is what happened, but there was a prior step at which the cause was seen in terms of the participants. The race of the Whites was, therefore, italicized instead of transcended.

At the same time, the White, because of his Whiteness, is considered to view the Negro in an equivalent way: Blackness precedes the signal. One student observed that White teachers "aren't trusted," because "they don't give them [students] a chance to prove themselves." Another reported: "I do not feel that I could trust a White man. I would always be afraid that he would, in some way, get to prove his assumptions about Negroes to be true."

The saliency of his Whiteness is not the only aspect of the Negro community with which the White is unfamiliar. These other aspects cause him to act in ways that make the Whiteness still more visible. When a teacher questioned fundamentalist religion, the students, according to one, responded with: "He's White and he's trying to undermine us." The teacher was challenging what amounted to anchors for the lives of his students, since religion has also been fundamental to the Negro in providing a defense against the White world. The gravity of the challenge, coupled with an existing mistrust, makes intentional "undermining" an obvious conclusion.

The White further succeeds in aggravating his awkwardness through attempts to define mistrust out of existence. These efforts generally take the form of redefining either the Negro or the White. However, one of the limitations to the approach is that it has not been standardized in a way that makes either variety of redefinition, or any one variety within the redefinition, appropriate for a particular occasion. This is because no exemption technique has been authorized by the Negro.

The Negro has located himself within what he intends to be an inapproachable place, much like the White has traditionally done vis-à-vis the Negro. The important difference is that Negroes have been able to gain admission to that place through *sub rosa* methods. Since the Movement White is trying to prove that he has the trust of the Negro, it would be an admission of his failure if he did not proceed in the open. He therefore provides himself with a plausible explanation for avoiding the open. In dealing with the spokesman for the mistrust instead of the target, the Negro cannot be confronted because, it is supposed, he could not afford to do anything but reject the redefinition.

The two approaches used by the White are closely connected. In order to redefine himself, the White must redefine the Negro. For the belief that an exemption is possible requires a prior assumption that the Negro is not to be taken literally. The White assumes himself able to inspect beneath the surface of the mistrust, and thereby uncover what he believes to be the true basis for the expressed hostility. The conclusion he seeks to reach is that what had appeared to be mistrust is actually caused by a factor that probably has no relevance to race, and surely has no relevance to himself.

But as an articulated statement, redefining the Negro comes later, because in most cases this redefinition, regardless of its accuracy, requires a feeling of better acquaintanceship with the Negro than redefining the White. Generally, then, it is the more experienced Whites who will redefine the Negro. An example arose when a White attending a civil rights conference determined that Whites were unwelcome and ought not to participate any further (in other words, he was able to recognize the relevance of the mistrust; hence he belongs to the next stage). He mentioned the idea to a White who had recently transferred to a Negro college and whose reply was based on a redefinition of Whites by categorizing them, with the implication he belonged to the beneficent group: "Are they afraid there are some outsiders . . . that someone will talk to Jim Clark [then the Sheriff of Dallas County, Alabama]?" A White who had been a transfer student for a longer time rejected the suggestion by redefining the Negro, whose mistrust appeared as no more than an unconsidered act: "It's just a matter of emotional impact."

Essentially, redefining the Negro is an attempt to see through him. The last White referred to above described his friendship with a Negro at college who suddenly stopped talking to him because "I have nothing to say to you, White man." The White dismissed it by noting the Negro "has got this thing with his father [an Army Colonel]." Similarly, a White was working in a civil rights organization when informed, "Goddamn Whites want to take everything over." This White explained away the accuser and therefore the accusation: "She doesn't know how to act so she does the opposite. She thinks that's how she's supposed to act. . . . It's very pitiful."

Or to state it another way, redefining the Negro is essentially an attempt to establish his motive. In getting at what he believes to be the source of the act or pronouncement, he finds an exemption from mistrust. One difficulty for the White in achieving an exemption conferred by the Negro, rather than by himself alone, is that Negroes also are concerned with motives. The difference is that they use the motives of the White as a means of substantiating their mistrust toward him. However, the White tries to overlook this scrutiny of his motives by temporarily giving a higher priority to his own interpretation. A Negro civil rights worker told a White volunteer, "You're down here to suffer a little; to do something for your ego." The White did not have to take this seriously, because: "Personally, I think he's ashamed that there aren't more Negroes in the Movement down here."

In order to assert his claim for an exemption, the White usually locates himself in a would-be trustworthy category by more than implication. Students at one school organized a meeting to discuss "How the White faculty is trying to take over." The clearly racial basis for the charges presented at the meeting did not prevent the attending White instructors from establishing what they considered safe categories for themselves. One teacher explained that neither race nor mistrust was involved; it was merely a misunderstanding caused by their being "newcomers," and "Northerners." In denying the accusation, this White was trying to offer a more viable basis for trust than Whiteness. As a newcomer, he is in an unfamiliar situation—without the knowledge to exercise dominance. As a Northerner, he is an ally of the Negro—without the inclination to exercise dominance.

An alternative to relocating oneself in a hopefully unobjectionable category is to remain in an objectionable one that has been redefined. This method includes a view from within of the terrors that exist where the nonresident assumes there is only comfort. It is in the nature of a confession, and enables the White to strengthen his feeling of kinship with the Negro by uncovering common bonds. One such approach appeared in a mimeographed document written by a civil rights worker who distributed copies to all staff members of the organization. A representative passage explained that "We middle-class Americans, the respectable, 'educated' people, are really confused. We keep repressing the natural and letting ourselves be ruled by the man-made, when the only sensible way to live is to create the man-made to satisfy the natural." In the larger context of her paper, she made it clear that, so far from "repressing the natural," the Negro *was* the natural; whatever else the Negro may be oppressed by, he is free of domination by "the man-made." Therefore the "middle-class Americans" (meaning Whites) are, according to the argument of that document, in bondage.

The most prevalent use of categories entails expanding them so that Whites and Negroes can be enveloped together, as in sharing bondage.[1] The usual method is to establish equivalence between the races. When one White who employed this kind of technique was asked his purpose, he stated that it was "an intellectual exercise"; but he eventually

---

[1] A similar technique is used by Indian instructors to deal with the opposite problem. Negroes tend to claim them, but they do not wish to be. The Indians therefore find categories that permit them to be subsumed with Whites. One explained that the location of the Caucasus Mountains means the Indians are Caucasians. According to another, Sanskrit manuscripts have established that Indians were originally Aryans.

realized that "it had unconscious racial implications." He went on to explain its purpose was "to contain him [a Negro presenting a case for mistrusting Whites], so he is less frightening—in order to understand him."

Expressions of nationalism lose their meaning when incorporated by equivalence. The objective of nationalism is to provide a basis for thought and action that is unique and, therefore, without equivalence. The White is able to make these expressions so relevant to himself, that they lose their intended relevance. When a visiting White instructor at a Negro college heard a definition of Black Power, he located it in "the liberal tradition . . . it's exactly what was said to [Oliver] Cromwell's officers."

At the same time, equivalence can mean the Negro loses some of his meaning for Whites. The climax of a play presented at a Negro college occurs when an elderly Negro sharecropper, one of the two characters, studies a portrait of Jesus and asks: "Why come haven't we made nothing that looks like us?"[2] At another point, his wife, who can bear nothing Black, explains that she murdered their only child "Because it would've been a nigger." During a discussion of the play afterwards, a White instructor described it as "A poor man's [Who's Afraid of] Virginia Woolf." To the extent nationalism, or any other barrier against intrusion by Whites, forces them to suppose the Negro is undergoing experiences that are no different from those in the White world, they are unable to romanticize the Negro.

When the Negro aims at a particular White, equivalence is also used for defusing. A White teacher who was charged with paternalism countered (privately, for it was prefaced by "I wanted to say"): "Talking about White paternalism, there's Negro paternalism. What difference does it make? It's just another kind of paternalism." A second White teacher, who planned to assign a novel by a Negro, was con-

[2] Gilbert Moses, Roots, in the repertory of the Free Southern Theatre.

fronted with "doubts whether I could teach it in a meaningful way; whether I could understand the human psychology
of it." She insisted that "If I couldn't [understand the Negro
novelist], the Negro student couldn't understand *Great Expectations,* or any book by a White." The versatility of equivalence lets the first White teacher discount the accusation
because it is applicable to Negroes, while the second teacher
can discount the accusation because it is not applicable to
Negroes.

One point at which these attempted exemptions fail
is before they are deployed. For the deployment does not
take place until a need for it is thought to exist; during the
lag between finding a need for the exemption technique and
formulating it, there is likely to be a fleeting recognition of
the mistrust. The internal contest was described by one civil
rights worker in this way: "I would begin to be conscious
[of the mistrust], but I'd fight it." When these fleeting recog-
nitions accumulate, they become an ongoing recognition.

After these deployments, it gradually becomes clear to
the White that they are more convincing to him than the
Negro. A White volunteer described his sacrifice, and concluded: "When blood flows, it's not black or white—it's red."
In an important sense, however, the Negro considers blood to
have a racial coloring. As a civil rights worker argued, "If I'm
killed, it's just another nigger; if you're White and killed,
maybe something might be done about it." (For evidence,
there is often cited the responsiveness of the President and the
Congress to the death of a White in Selma, and their un-
responsiveness to the death of a Negro in the same period and
vicinity.)

Economic deprivation supplies the most frequent attempt at establishing a state of mutual oppression with the
Negro. It offers a common past: "If you look at history, it's
lower classes in general that have suffered. My folks are from
there [Appalachia], some of it's bad as any of the Negro

tenant shacks in Georgia." For another White, it offers a common present: "The Man's foot is on my back as long as I'm broke." On hearing one such argument, a Negro observed: "That's a lot of crap."

A fuller, but equivalent, response was received from a Negro, who had been emphasizing the term "black communities," after he was asked: "What would your reaction be to calling these communities 'Movement communities'—on a multi-racial basis, to absorb the drop-outs from the White community?" The Negro replied that "The Black community is the poor community . . . [White people, with] all their experiences and what they consider natural, are not from that community. . . . Those who don't suffer must be prepared to listen and not to play an active role."

The creation of categories not only fails to convince the Negro, it can highlight the unacceptability of a White, as when alienation is used as a theme of equivalence: "[Negroes] say Whites don't know what it's like to be Black. . . . A lot of Negroes don't know what it's like to be a White trying to work in a civil rights group and being alienated; as well as being alienated from their own group. It's hard to realize that too." One White who used an alienation appeal was told by a Negro that there was a difference: Whites were alienated "by choice." Only members of an establishment can opt to become outsiders. (This is not to say the other insiders and existing outsiders will grant the option.)

The way in which these appeals are stated can incriminate the White as much as their content. When Whites were condemned by the Negro members of a civil rights organization, a White responded: "I maintain that regardless of the color of our skin, we're all Black. We're all on the same team . . . fighting the Eastlands." One of the condemning Negroes turned to another and, in reference to the speaker, irreverently replied: "Bless you."

The Negro frequently relies on categories to establish

the untrustworthiness of the White. After a White civil rights worker described her efforts "to get some kind of political motivation in the [Negro] community," she was asked if there "is any room in your community for Negroes to help White people?" Equivalence is used as a way of demonstrating that none exists.

Categories are arranged by the Negro in ways that vary enough to be the reverse of each other. His approach from one direction is to assign all Whites to a single enveloping category, in order to show there is no room for exemptions; the responsibility is shared equally among Whites, as an audience of them was told, in spite of, or *a fortiori* because of, disavowals:

> *Life* magazine had a picture of the people who did the murder; and they picture them eating, and laughing, and joking, and talking as though they were morally idiots. I think most people in the country reading that got that impression. But you don't put yourself in that classification so they're other people—they're not like you, or like us. *The Saturday Evening Post* had a picture of a Ku Klux Klan on the front page just recently, and at the end of the article talked about them as outcasts, as people who are in no way like most Americans, as rejects from the society. I think that's a false interpretation which people are getting, and, therefore, they analyze the problem wrongly, and, therefore, they look for wrong solutions.

His approach from the other direction is to establish various classifications of Whites, in order to show there is no room for exemptions. The White is presented as a bundle of relationships with the Negro. Each category of relationship includes all Whites as oppressors and all Negroes as oppressed. Rentier was one of several categories presented by another Negro while addressing a group of White civil workers; he reminded them that they were not the free agents they supposed: "We're raising some good questions, but are we willing to talk to it? How much land do your parents own?"

When a White civil rights worker went into a Negro slum he found himself isolated for being "an insurance collector." In this case, the Negroes did not know who he "really" was, but even if they should know, it has little effect on the category already chosen. Upon asking a Negro from the local, nonacademic, community how he thought it would react to his dating one of its young women, a White instructor was told, "They might think you're the son of a plantation owner; just down here to see how much you could get." As in this case, it is even more important to have the White classified in familiar terms (which are the ones initially applied) after it is known who he "really" is, or more accurately, who he is not, because this makes it easier to deal with him.

The one or more categories chosen by the Negro usually reveal, since they result from, his particular preoccupations. A graphic case arose when a Negro minister stated at the chapel service on a campus: "It is a shame that our students are being led astray by White carpet-baggers from the North." On previous occasions he had defended Southern Whites, so that it was appropriate for him to use what was originally their term as a means of describing White faculty. While for a student who was a civil rights activist, the teacher appeared as "a White cracker from the North."

Although the categories used by Whites have none of the intended effect on the Negro, the categories that the Negro uses have a considerable effect on Whites. For whether or not the White is from a land-owning family, this and similar assumptions eventually provide him with a vivid sense of his Whiteness. As he learns, partly through these categories, what his Whiteness means to the Negro, he moves on to the next stage.

Meanwhile, moving to the present stage has been a

gradual process. This movement has been assisted, and delayed, by discovering the emoluments of race. To admit they exist is first, an acknowledgement that Whiteness exists, and next, that Whiteness cannot be transcended by good intentions. In short, the process of discovery is the same as that for mistrust. For these rewards are the substance of Whiteness and consequently of mistrust. The final discovery is that exemption from the emoluments will not be granted. Because regardless of how he sees himself, "You share in the benefits of the White man."

At the outset, the White is oblivious to his power, which is made tangible by those emoluments. While orienting a group of White volunteers for work in the South, a Negro civil rights worker warned of the unwitting, but regular, uses of this power by Whites working in Negro communities. He cited the case of a White girl who was working with a voting registration project. The canvassers needed a car. One day she announced having found one for $500, but was reminded the project could not even afford the gas. She therefore telephoned her father for the money and he wired it. The Negroes on the project were demoralized by this display of what he described as "power."

While the White earlier considered it necessary to substantiate the assurance component of his indignation by emphasizing what he regarded as his contribution to the Movement, it now begins to appear that a de-emphasis is necessary to achieve an exemption. A White student at a Southern White college told a civil rights conference how much he and other students accomplished by organizing the Negro maids at the school. On hearing his account of their activity, a Negro civil rights worker commented: "You see where that's going: it's reinforcing old myths." The White later remarked, "I had never really thought about it until today. Maybe it's different at _____. We don't want any power. There's nothing we could do with it."

When the White finds himself holding a position of power within the Movement, he seeks to redefine it. A White who was made supervisor of printing for a civil rights organization explained, "I wasn't the supervisor, I was just one step in front of [Negroes] on the assembly line; somebody had to do the creating." In the previous case, it was thought sufficient to establish equality with those who were nominally subordinates. But when a White was given broader power, through an administrative position at a Negro college, equality was not enough, or rather, it was too much; he told an interviewer for the campus newspaper:

> As I think of my position as Acting Dean, I find myself humming that old standard: "If That Isn't Love." The way that Fats Waller sang it back in the 30's and 40's, the lyric went, slightly paraphrased, like this: I'll work for you, I'll slave for you, I'll be a beggar or a knave for you, and if that's not a Dean it'll have to do until the real thing comes along.

The largest problem comes after Whites realize these disclaimers must be proven to the Negro. It is one thing to say, as a White activist in Mississippi did, that "I'm here to lose my power"; to make it convincing is another matter. Acting out the disclaimer is more complicated than relying on restated categories. For these actions must contend with a way of life that provides the emoluments with reality. A White learned this while working for a civil rights organization located in the Negro section of a Southern city. When he waited to cross a main street at the middle of the block near the office, he found the drivers, who were Negroes, always stopped for him. He concluded this was an acknowledgement of his race. Thereafter, he went out of his way to cross at the corner with the light.

The White does not always have this much control over whether he will be the beneficiary of racial distinctions.

Another, more experienced, White civil rights worker who was trying to organize maids finally concluded there was no way he could succeed, for whenever he tried to discuss the union with the maids, the response was "Yes sir, yes sir." He found himself an agent of the dominance from which he was trying to free them. A White working in a different Southern community encountered the same problem during a voting registration drive. She then tried to persuade the local high school students that they should learn how to say "yes" without adding "sir" by practicing on the White civil rights workers.

But this accommodation is not simply a matter of language. A suggestion of its depth arose in response to a White who asked a Negro civil rights worker whether her work in a Negro community was "antagonizing the whole situation? Is there any place for Whites there?" He replied: "We have Whites on our staff, but they have to recognize what it means when a little girl strokes their long blonde hair." She asked: "Is that antagonizing?" He then explained, "It's perpetuating."

Racial emoluments are imposed on the civil rights worker by Southern Whites as well as Negroes. It is most likely to occur in jail, since this is the only place where the White segregationist and desegregationist have sustained contact with each other. The White civil rights workers often find themselves arrested with the Negroes but then separated in jail and sometimes provided with amenities, such as mattresses, that are denied Negro prisoners. The White prisoners then usually demand that they be allowed to desegregate the cells occupied by Negroes (significantly, not that Negroes be moved into White cells). These demands are accompanied by protests involving hunger strikes or other methods that deny them the necessities that the Negroes have.

Forsaken emoluments may result in vindicating mistrustful Negroes. The inviolability of White womanhood is an example. White female civil rights workers tend to assume that by making themselves sexually available to Negroes, they will demonstrate an acceptance that, in turn, entitles them to acceptance. A more likely result is open hostility from the local Negro women. Their initial assumption, later proven to their satisfaction, is suggested by the women in one community who insisted that the White females were there because "They ran out of White men." Similar conflicts developed in a civil rights organization among the staff. The hostility of Negro female workers reached a level that required their organization to hold a "retreat" for them one week, and for the White female workers another week. An attraction to the White woman that was intensified through her unapproachability can now be acted on by Negro men, so that her power is demonstrated more formidably than if she remained aloof.

Even where Whites are aware of having power in an abstract sense, there is no assurance they can recognize what the Negro considers its concrete forms. The recognition is more difficult when, in the abstract, there is nothing racial about these concrete forms. Typing, for instance, acquires a racial significance when, as pointed out by a Negro, Whites in a civil rights project "know how to type, so they do it"; with the result that Negroes, who are unable to type, "feel insecure."

It is not so much what Whites do or do not do about their power, as what they signify. The following observations were made by a Negro about the civil rights project that a predominantly White organization had initiated:

> Do they [the Negroes in the surrounding community] notice the Whites have got that organization? Whites have run everything else. Maybe the Whites do a lot of decision-making. Maybe they [the Negroes] see that. Maybe they imagine it, because that's the way it's always been. So they stay away from it, or don't trust it.

Moreover, the White is continually judged by fictive base lines. As a student commented about the White faculty, "Sometimes I wonder whether they teach us the same way they would at a White school. They might think: 'I can water it down, because they'll comply with anything I say.'" The same wondering extends to the extracurricular activities of White faculty members. When a touring (White) ballet performed on a campus, the White faculty members who attended were dressed, according to one student, "informally . . . just because it's [the Negro College]." It was assumed that they would have dressed less informally on a White campus. More pointedly, a student suggested that White faculty "come South because these people want to be themselves, and they hope that among tolerant, poor, culturally deprived Blacks they can be the way they think they really are."

The power of Whiteness is implicit here; reflected in what is considered to be its by-product: disrespect. Before reaching this conclusion, the Negro has put the behavior of Whites amongst Whites in the best possible light. In order to do so, it is sometimes necessary to overlook White-to-White contact that is observable; as one Negro instructor said about others who appraised a White administrator: "They can forget that he's aggressive towards Whites, and that's exactly what happens."

The alternative base line, putting the behavior of Whites amongst Whites in its worst possible light, occurs when there is no observable and discreditable behavior towards Negroes. In these circumstances, it is assumed that Whites act, unlike the above case, "the way they think they really are" only when in the company of Whites. Here, power takes an explicit form. The encounters are no less vivid to the Negro for being hypothetical. A White instructor complained to a Negro colleague: "I try to be friendly, and you're so aloof." The Negro replied: "I don't want to get too close, because you might turn White and then I'd get hurt." His examples of "White" occurred outside of the campus orbit. For instance, being seen downtown by the White who would "ignore me." Similarly, a student told his White teacher: "If you and I went to a restaurant, and I couldn't get in, you would go in anyway." Or, as one student summarized it for another, "They grin with you here, and forget out there." (The outside contact with Whites can also be a revelation to the White. While shopping, a teacher "reached for a can of tomatoes on a shelf when all of a sudden I realized the people around were a pinkish-white, with blue veins showing on white legs—it was very unappetizing. I realized that must be how I look to the students at _____.")

By borrowing gauges from the White community, the Negro is protected from what he considers an attempt to mislead him about the nature of equality. Referring to those who become teachers, a student asked: "Isn't it typically White for a few Whites of 'the true humanitarian spirit' to low-rate themselves to our level, so we can say we are 'equal'?" In order for the White to succeed in this fabrication of equality that results from bringing himself down to the level of the Negro, rather than by bringing the Negro up to his level, it is assumed he first tries to make certain the world of his origin is beyond the sight of the Negro. Yet, the Negro further assumes that the White expects to profit from his stay in the Negro community to the extent its members are aware of an exalted White world from which he is an emissary. For as another student pointed out: "White instructors come here with the idea that since they are supposedly from a superior race they will get a higher position in a Negro institution than in a White institution."

To counteract assumptions that he is asserting his power, the White engages in deference, or tries to at any rate. As viewed by the Negro, the deference of Whites is characterized by dominance. Accordingly, what is deference to the White is paternalism to the Negro.

Paternalism usually arises when the White does what

the Negro does not want to be compelled to accept, but would like done for him if he could compel the White to do it. The content of this deference makes it clear to the Negro that the White is initiating it from a base of superiority. For the White provides goods and services generally unavailable from Negroes. At the same time, it serves to remind the Negro of the source of his inferiority.

Through deference, the White makes allowances for the other being Negro. He is also making allowances for being White. A White instructor described his policy toward cheaters, and then observed: "Maybe I bend over backwards because I'm White. Because of their background, it's important they think we believe them." If both parties were Negro, so that allowances for the other were being made in a context of trust, the evaluation would be altered. The donor of deference would not have to make allowances for himself. Moreover, the donee would not regard it as paternalism; instead, it would become loyalty.

Since the Negro has declined to provide the White with guidelines for obtaining trust, deference appears as a likely course of action. It seems to the White that deference has been indirectly sanctioned for the purpose by Negroes. After all, they have traditionally used deference to gain the trust of White folks. But this is still another reason why Negroes consider it objectionable. For as used by Negroes, deference has provided a way to violate that trust with safety.

Paternalism is thought to intensify the conditions that produced it. The office of a civil rights organization in Mississippi was regularly visited by young Negroes who asked the White volunteers for money, and received it. Finally, the Negro civil rights workers told the Whites to stop, because "You're making niggers out of them."

Since paternalism is considered a means of giving to the Negro with an end of taking from him, it is seen in terms of its expected results. For one student, referring to the proffered hospitality of a White teacher and his wife, the form taken by these results was clear, even if their content was not: "They're always asking me over there; they always seem to be trying to get something out of me—I don't know what." The students usually have a more exact idea of what the White faculty is trying to get out of them. As seen by another student, it was acceptance: "They would invite me out to their homes for dinner. . . . I began to wonder why they were so nice to me. I arrived at the conclusion that they were trying to exploit and use me . . . . It's better for them to act like they care since they're in a predominantly Negro institution."

Deference has the simultaneous effect of showing Negroes how the White wants them to be dependent on him, and how they can thwart this supposed intention. For the types of dependence that the White is seen trying to elicit first require the compliance of the Negro. In this way, the White is dependent on the Negro during the first phase, which the Negro tries to prolong so he will not have to encounter a second phase.

A Negro instructor says the indulgence of the White faculty member means that "Instead of helping the students to grow and develop, he's preparing them to have their heads broken." In other words, the White is not preparing the student for the real world where, according to a second Negro teacher, "The Civil Rights Law says discrimination is illegal, but it can't make a man hire someone." This teacher believes the White instructor is "replacing one kind of paternalism with another kind of paternalism . . . by wining and dining and draining them dry, he's making them dependent on him—like the Southern White man."

The mistrust is more dramatic when harbored by the recipients of this indulgence—the students. One of them noted, "Negroes know about all the hell they caught, and in order to get us prepared they must give us hell now. In the situation with the White instructor, most of them just don't care. They are like many White Southerners. They want to keep you down and they are doing this by what we call 'being easy.'" An equally dramatic example of trust occurs, as here, when it is directed against one who has been acting harshly. (This is not to say Negro instructors are exempted from racial condemnations by the students; but when one is criticized, it is because he "thinks he's White." In one case, a student noted that when her Negro instructor "talks about Negroes, instead of using 'we,' she uses 'y'all.'")

The White teacher, as well as the Negro student and instructor, finds a connection between his indulgence and the White Southerner. But where the Negro sees the indulgence as an extension of traditional racism, the White teacher sees it as a repudiation. A White explained that he had acted permissively toward a student who had cheated, because "If you say 'No,' what are you saying? You're saying they're a liar. They get that from White policemen." (One of the rare guidelines available to the Movement White is provided by White segregationists. Even where he has had no contact with known racists, he finds it easier to anticipate them than to anticipate the Negro with whom he has had considerable contact. The assumption is that the Negro would want a White to act opposite from the way in which racists do, so that the guideline results from reversing their expected behavior. However, this guideline replaces one form of awkwardness with another. For although it gives the Movement White a framework, it demands he put himself in the place of a racist.

LABORATORY OF EXEMPTION-SEEKING

In evaluating the White teacher, students at Negro colleges generally minimize his occupation in order to maximize his race. Through an attempt to minimize his race, the White teacher tries to minimize his occupation, because he believes the traditional relationship between White and Negro resembles the relationship between teacher and student, irrespective of race. That is, the teacher, like the White, has a position of dominance. (The second part of this equation is not discovered until the next stage; it then becomes clear that the Negro, like the student, has traditionally found covert means of undermining this dominance.) The White teacher therefore assumes that his occupation compounds the burden imposed by his race. Moreover, the assumption continues, in the process of removing the barriers separating teacher from students, he will demonstrate his contempt for superordination, and thus provide grounds for exemption from Whiteness. Accordingly, the White teacher at a Negro school tends to do everything possible to eliminate the attributes of authority that are associated with teaching.

As the most ubiquitous reminder of authority, rules are the most consistent target of the White instructor. By disregarding the formal and informal rules of teaching, he tries to reject the rules of race relations. In not taking class attendance, for example, the rejection is symbolic; it is an effort to announce that he wants a conspiracy with the students—rather than by or against them. But the rejected rules may also have a more direct connection with race, as when he prevents students from addressing him as "Mr." If used by the students he has contact with outside of class, one teacher tells them "Stop it!" In class he is more circuitous, but equally determined to abolish the courtesy title applied to his name; his efforts consist of "trying to find out where they're at, and getting them to talk to each other and to me."

The only rules that he observes are those that elevate the position of the student, and consequently reduce his distance from the instructor. This is particularly true when the elevation has a distinctly racial nature. Again, the case of "Mr." is relevant. The same teachers that reject its usage by students are equally rigorous in applying it to students.

The students are not always as anxious to ignore the rules, again both formal and informal, that apply to them. The following excerpts are from the journal of a student who had visited a class where the teacher was trying to establish informality; here are the obstacles at the beginning and end:

> After [the teacher] sat down, he told the students to move their desks around him. One boy said, "He's always asking us to sit around him. He's been saying this as long as we've been here, and yet some of the students sit in the back." . . . Finally the discussion, or I could say "trilogue" was over. [The teacher] said, "I'd be happy to stay and talk some more." Immediately one student replied, "No, that won't be necessary."

The White teacher is reminded of his membership in a racially superordinate group by the refusal of students to subordinate themselves to his wishes.

At the same time, students are reminded of his membership by his attempts to dissolve it. One technique for reducing the distance from students resulted in this comment: "Some [White] instructors openly show the prejudice they have for the Negroes by the smutty remarks which they make in class." The prejudice they are thought to be showing is of two kinds. First, the traditional prejudice of the Southern White that is considered another source of disrespect, especially where sexual matters are concerned. A student explained that "smutty remarks" inescapably involve prejudice "because things have been like this before." The second kind of ascribed prejudice takes a more modern form, inasmuch as it is considered peculiar to White faculty members. Since they are thought to be undergoing less of a migration than an excursion, they are in the nature of tourists, which means the students see themselves being seen as tourist attractions. Accordingly, the same student supposed the remarks of the teachers result from a curiousity "to see their [students'] reactions."

Another source of resistance is the Negro faculty, whose situation is the reverse of the White faculty. It needs to be accepted by the administration, but not by the students. As a rule, when the Negro teacher thinks of advancement, it is within the particular Negro college at which he is employed. He therefore needs the approval of the administration, an approval that depends heavily upon observing formal and informal rules. If anything, the Negro faculty overextend rules, creating them where none exist. One Negro instructor provided his undergraduate classes with mimeographed instructions stating, in part, that term papers had to be prefaced with "In partial fulfillment of the requirements for. . . ." Negro faculty are, for the most part, isolated from the larger educational establishment to a point where they are somewhat uncertain how to procede in accord with it; it is their model, but often dimly seen (the professional organizations to which they belong are usually run by and for Negroes). Rules, however much their distortion reflects this isolation, provide some measure of security.

Because the White faculty member generally sees the Negro college as the beginning of his career or as an interlude in it, not as its culmination, no administrative sanction is relevant to him. The administration, as the propagator and enforcer of rules, is considered a worthy target by the White faculty: "Fighting the Administration is like fighting the White man." Further, if the White instructor feels uncomfortable about the academic establishment, it is because he has, in most cases, been so much a part of it, and is now seeking freedom from it, especially its rules.

The variation in approach to rules was seen when two faculty members entered a campus bookstore that required all customers to remove their overcoats as a means of discouraging shoplifting. The Negro complied; the White teacher ignored the request and later said he was "hoping they would make an issue out of it, because I was going to raise hell."

While eliminating rules because of racial implications,

the same White faculty members work equally hard at introducing a more overt form of race into their classrooms for the same object of exempting themselves from Whiteness. The approach consists of presenting documentation, usually by Negro novelists, that the White man is the enemy.[3] Such efforts by the White instructor are calculated to demonstrate his trustworthiness. They first of all declare that he sees the White man as he believes the students do. There is also the strong inference that he and they share this enemy. As proof, there is the acknowledgement itself. For if he were not an ally, he believes it plain that he could not afford to introduce a subject that might implicate him. In return, he wants the students to demonstrate their trust of him by acknowledging what he believes they would conceal from all other Whites— that all other Whites are the enemy.

In addition to seeking exemptions, the approaches based on an elimination and a brandishing of race resemble each other in the matter of rules. The traditional didactic rules, as applied to course material and an interpretation of it, would (in all but the social sciences) prevent an approach that emphasized the social issues of race. This is one reason that the approach is discouraged by the Negro faculty members. The Negro chairman of a freshman English program

[3] On another level, the overlapping of race and occupation is a legacy from the early White teachers. These missionaries (as they were in fact, or—to Whites, at least—honorifically) acted from a stance that one referred to as "noblesse oblige." (Samuel Chapman Armstrong, quoted in Francis Greenwood Peabody, *Education for Life: The Story of Hampton Institute*, Garden City, N.Y., Doubleday, Page and Co., 1918, p. 210.) Accordingly, they defined their teaching responsibilities broadly: "We are trying to teach cleanliness as well as reading and spelling, but it is a tough job, for the poor creatures have lived so long in a filthy condition that they don't know what it is to be clean." (Mary Ames, *From A New England Woman's Diary in Dixie in 1865*, Springfield, Mass., no publisher, 1906, pp. 25–26.) As they saw it, then, teaching Negroes meant indoctrinating them with White virtues. So, to the extent the current White teachers try to make their students Black, and insofar as these instructors try to do the same for themselves, they are dissociating themselves from the traditional Northern White teacher—the missionary.

sent a memorandum that contained the following to its faculty (the horrible examples referred to are White instructors):

> . . . imitation [of literary examples] helps one to improve his style of writing. Frequently teachers who find it too difficult to teach composition will lapse into teaching impressionistic literary criticism or a Criticism of Life by way of *The Adventures of Huckleberry Finn*. I don't think they should. I think they should teach composition no matter how difficult and boring it may be. —— employs teachers whose primary responsibility it is to preside over the student's main learning experience in literature; the college employs us to preside over the basic writing experience of first-year students. When we convert Communications 101 and Communications 101A into discussions of Great Ideas (or How to Like What I Like), we subvert the objective of the courses.

The ascendancy of messages over rules became more explicit when a White English instructor provided his class with transcripts of a Freedom School session. The Negro instructor at the Freedom School had begun by writing typical phrases of the local residents on the left side of the board ("The peoples want freedom"); on the right side, he wrote the grammatical equivalent ("The people want freedom"). The White teacher made it clear to his composition class that he agreed with the concluding remark of a young Negro who appeared in the transcript: "If the majority speaks on the left [of the blackboard], then a minority must rule society. Why do we have to change to be accepted by the minority group? If I change for society, I wouldn't be free anyway."

The simultaneous methods of the White faculty also share the fact that they do not have the intended results. After his first year, a History instructor lamented: "They just wouldn't admit the White is the enemy." Whites and Negroes appearing to identify with each other might sound like the basis for a racial idyll. In fact, it produces a racial conflict, as an English instructor discovered while discussing *That Evening Sun* by William Faulkner. She felt Jason had a "terrifying knowledge of how to use Negroes." Whereas the students "sympathized with him and felt he wasn't being understood" by others in the novel, including the Negroes.[4] Another English teacher used a source that, on paper at least, was more relevant to the class: *Invisible Man* is by a former student at the college who describes it in vivid detail. But it, too, was a protest novel to the teacher and an affirmation novel to the students. To support his interpretation of the book, the teacher asked the class about the significance of a dream sequence in which the protagonist is told by his grandfather

> to open my brief case and read what was inside and I did, finding an official envelope stamped with the state seal; and inside the envelope I found another and another, endlessly, and I thought I would fall of weariness. "Them's years," he said. "Now open that one." And I did and in it I found an engraved document containing a short message in letters of gold. "Read it," my grandfather said. "Out loud."
>
> "To Whom It May Concern," I intoned. "Keep This Nigger-Boy Running."[5]

[4] If some kind of base line were to appear for measuring the content of fiction, it would probably turn out that here the White instructor overstates the racial significance in one direction as much as the students understate it in the other direction. Jason is five years old; the one Negro, Nancy, that he has more than the briefest contact with is actually taking advantage of him, by using him as a buffer against the anticipated vengeance of her husband. Since Nancy is nominally the servant of Jason, it can be said there is a racial significance here, but it takes a form that would work against the particular case for which the White instructor is seeking evidence.

[5] Ralph Ellison, *Invisible Man,* New York, New American Library (Signet Books), 1953, pp. 34–35.

Only one student was willing to commit herself; she explained that it meant, "If at first you don't succeed—try, try again."

It is not because the analysis offered by White faculty is inaccurate that the students are unable to accept it, but because it often approaches accuracy. The background to being thus threatened is contained in the following comment of a Negro student who has had several White teachers:

> This is supposed to be a haven from race; it's just like a bird sanctuary. When someone asks "Is that an all Negro college?" you're offended, because you never thought of it that way. They have a mutual understanding: "If you won't say anything about it, I won't." There's no place to go, so they're not going to let you tell them that everything is not milk and honey. [As opposed to rural Negroes who drop out of high school because their view of the world is:] "All I know is picking cotton; all I'm going to know is picking cotton." They don't have anything to go to school for. I've been brought up believing if I go to college, I can make it. Now you give me a book; it takes three hours to read. It's three hours against eighteen years. [Should Negro instructors use novels by Negroes it would be to demonstrate that] "If they try a little harder, they'll make it. Educational qualifications are the way out of all that misery." [Whites] teach that it's a definite problem: "Just because you're a Negro, you have three strikes against you; the whole world's against you."

In other words, the White instructor who characteristically believed he had failed in trying "to bring the material closer to the kids" was wrong. He has brought the material too close to them, so close that the variety and persistence of their defenses appear in the following excerpts from book reports for White teachers:

Invisible Man. "This book especially appeals to me because it represents the invisibility of the Negro and man as a whole."

A Raisin in the Sun. ". . . with faith, understanding and combined efforts many obstacles may be overcome."

Huckleberry Finn. "[Huck] seemed truly devoted to Jim. He knew that Jim was just [sic] a servant but this didn't seem to affect his feelings in any way."

Black Like Me. "This book was very meaningful to me because I didn't realize people were still trying to live and being treated as they were in the South." [By a native of Alabama.]

To Kill a Mockingbird. "I liked the novel so well because it pointed out that Negroes, Whites and other groups cannot be classified as good or bad."

Othello. "I like this piece of literature because it showed that Shakespeare was not discriminatory in his writing."

The ingenuity of the White teacher in introducing racial themes is suggested by this question from an Economics examination:

You are a Negro leader who has been elected to decide fiscal and monetary measures to take for the purpose of economic stability. You are aware that increases in the price level hurt low income Negro groups, whose incomes remain stable while prices rise. You are also aware that a downturn will cause unemployment to the Negro group in the population. From your knowledge of the economics of the situation can you as the policy maker avoid antagonizing the Negroes?

The greater ingenuity of the student in circumventing the apparently unavoidable need for a racial decision appeared in this conclusion of a typical answer:

If these two means did not work, I would be in a
dilemma as to what to do next that would be in the
best interest not only to Negroes but to the whole econ-
omy.

These answers cause the White teacher to use these
assignments and examinations for a more basic objective than
establishing grounds for his exemption. He finds it necessary
to reassure himself that those to whom he is applying for an
exemption are in fact Negroes, as he has conceptualized
them. Before this reassurance is possible, he finds it necessary
to instruct them in the ways of Blackness.

Misled by their racial neutrality, the White instructor
does manage to activate the race consciousness of his students.
It is directed against him—not just other Whites, for he does
not recognize that there is a point beyond which only the
Negro can go with race consciousness. This fact combines
with the uneasy commitment of his students to the Democratic Ideal, as described above. The White instructor,
then, alternately generates too much Whiteness and too much
Blackness. The result is that students assume he is trying to
further subjugate them. One student observed that "Most of
them [students] feel as though they [White instructors] want
to keep Negroes down because they always want them to
read those novels about how the Negro had a hard time, such
as *Invisible Man* and Baldwin."

There is nothing vague about the goal of trust that
White faculty members expect to attain by eliminating de-
marcations, for the need to belong that it can fulfill is vivid.
In their minds, the most direct route to belonging is through
the Movement, since it best expresses their investment in the
Negro. They also consider teaching to be inseparable from
the Movement when the classroom is used as a forum for
racial agitprop. Moreover, the White faculty, unlike the Negro faculty, does not have a ready-made community through

such preexisting connections as membership in college fraternities that inevitably have an active adult chapter in the
vicinity. One White faculty member at a Negro college felt
discriminated against because promotions seemed to revolve
around such membership. A Negro instructor who observed
the recent desegregation of the faculty at his college thought
the resistance to Whites resembled in some ways what he and
others encountered at the same school thirty-five years earlier
when they arrived to provide the first liberal arts instruction.
The resisting faculty members were threatened by their degrees, they resented their higher salaries, and accused them
of being "newcomers." An important variation from the current hostility is that in spite of their differences, "There were
all kinds of formal and informal ties." As a result, the established faculty did not isolate the recent arrivals, as now happens to those who are White; "They invited us to their homes
and tried to indoctrinate us with the philosophy of [the Negro founder]." The contrast between these two periods of
transition bears a more distinctly racial aspect. The earlier
wave of instructors did not provoke sentiment such as the
Negro instructor currently heard with regularity: "The Negro
college has been one of the few things the Negro has had of
his own; and now they're trying to take that over."

Initially, efforts are made to obtain the friendship of
Negro faculty. Largely through the efforts of their wives
(who are less able to seek comraderie with the students), married White instructors pursue this objective furthest. But as
a Negro teacher said about one such quest: "I wanted to tell
him [a White family] tried it, and it didn't work. They'll reject him anyway. Maybe it's his way of solving the problem
[of being White]."

Associating with nonacademic Whites is not a solution. Local Whites are usually hostile; where contact is possible, the resultant hostility of campus Negroes is either a
reality or anticipated. Another recourse was tried by a faculty
couple who visited what they described as "liberal" friends

from the North who had moved South; the entire weekend was spent defending the Negroes at their college from the stereotypes held by their friends. Through default, the White faculty members have each other for a community. But this is unsatisfactory since it provides a continuous reminder of their exclusion from the Negro community.

Rejection by Negro instructors is unwelcome, although dismissable on the grounds that they, together with the administration, are still another common enemy of the White instructor and the students. The students are by no means so expendable to the White faculty. Yet, the White faculty is as expendable to the students as it is to the Negro faculty. Through the usual campus organizations and activities, students have their own world. This self-sufficiency does not discourage the White faculty members from selecting students as the means to a community.

The students are given this responsibility for a variety of reasons. First, they, far more than the Negro faculty, are seen as embodying those aspects of the Negro which attracted the White to the college. For instance, they are involved in civil rights activity (actually, only a small minority of any student body is involved on a continuing basis, but it is this minority to which the White faculty is drawn). Second, many of the White instructors are on leave from graduate work or have just completed it. Thus their experience and frame of reference are less those of faculty than of students. Third, they are not ordinarily expected to stay at the Negro college for more than a few years. Therefore, not only past, but present experience gives them an affinity with students; they are both defined as transients. In varying degrees these three factors are acknowledged by the White faculty. The fourth element is not likely to be, for it is based on the availability of students; they are a captive audience, but as it turns out, only in a very limited and misleading sense.

By removing boundaries, the White teacher seeks to

enter sectors that are more likely to raise the question of trustworthiness. The pervasive relationship sought by the White instructor has been described by a student: "He is not asking to be just a teacher; he's asking to be a teacher, counsellor, and friend." Since these additional sectors are much closer to the vital interests of the students, they are more private, and are protected accordingly.

To the extent White faculty members succeed in penetrating the conventions of Negro-White relations, the mistrust directed against them increases. One such occasion occurred at the apartment of a White instructor during a party he was giving for his acquaintances, which meant it was mainly attended by students. There were a few Whites present, half of them in the kitchen, half in the living room. Suddenly, one of the Negro students announced that the host was "a segregationist," because "Whenever I come here, all the Whites are in the kitchen." More important than whether the stated grounds for mistrust are present, the opportunity for expressing it is. For most students, the instructor is the first White that can be openly mistrusted. As a result of providing a safe target, the mistrust toward him is cumulative; he serves as a surrogate for all those less vulnerable Whites that the Negro has known.

The usual extracurricular enterprise of the White teacher is the seminar. Although intended to "reach" the student, it uses techniques that are the opposite from those he employs in the classroom for this purpose. It meets at the home of the instructor in the evening or on Sundays, but it also relies on texts and assignments. The seminar converts a customarily nonacademic setting into an academic one; whereas his campus courses convert a customarily academic setting into a nonacademic one. One such seminar mirrored the aspirations of its founder through the title: Center for Revolutionary Studies. The texts he assigned included such varied condemnations of the White as *Blues People* and *Facing Mt. Kenya*. The enrollment was to be comprised of former students whom he thought, from their prior contact in campus courses, accepted him. But none of those invited attended. At this point, the White instructor suddenly realized "how ready they are to put you on."

One of the invited students later said, in effect, that this had been the case. By summing up the philosophy of his classmates, he suggested the Center for Revolutionary Studies was based on an idealization of the student: "You don't come to college to think and develop ideas, you come to drink and have a good time." In courses for which they received credit and grades, there was a need to give the same teacher a false impression of rapport: "Those opinions are not his opinions, they're the opinions he thinks the teacher wants him to have." The discrepancy between what the students said and believed corresponds to a discrepancy on the part of the teacher when one of his techniques for eliminating Whiteness conflicted with another. He tried to be "the first White man they [the students] disagree with," but one of his students, according to another, "wrote a paper against Black Power [the assigned topic], and she was given a failing grade, and her paper was marked up. She said she guessed that after this she couldn't or wouldn't write what she actually felt, but what he wanted her to." In another case, a student privately described LeRoi Jones as "ain't shit," but she wrote about him enthusiastically, because the teacher "was trying to identify with Negroes."

This instructor was sufficiently unattuned to the nature of mistrust that he did not see it when it existed and finally saw it where there was none. He was unaware, for instance, that his offer to be faculty advisor of a student civil rights group was received with mistrust. But through his experience with the seminar he became aware of mistrust, although its failure was not, as he supposed, the result of mistrust.

By emphasizing racial themes, the White teacher establishes one form of inequality through his efforts to overcome another form of it. He becomes the disadvantaged member of the classroom. After an instructor initiated a Negro History course, a student commented: "We're on the inside track of that; how can she understand it?" Courses that are not officially racial, for example, one in Philosophy, elicit the same kind of response: "I wonder why he talks about Negroes all the time. He's always speaking as if he's one himself. I've been one all my life, and he can't tell me anything." So that when the White teacher finally does transcend his occupation, it is at the price of emphasizing his race. After it became known that an off-campus seminar would be supplemented with liquor and marijuana, students appeared. The assignments of anti-White literature and the discussion topics were ignored. But the guests talked among themselves, and while listening, the teacher discovered he had become the student: "The tables were turned . . . [I learned] how much the Negro hates and distrusts anything White." It was the teacher who had been reached.

COLLAPSE OF EXEMPTION-SEEKING

In order for the Negro to reach the White, he must penetrate an offense that takes the form of indignation, and then a defense that takes the form of awkwardness. An undermining of the defense appears in the tendency to make steadily greater concessions to the argument of the Negro.

Although not considered concessions by either of the parties involved, they arise, for example, where the Whites settle for becoming Negro by proxy. Members of a predominantly White civil rights group were, according to one of them, seen by the local community as "outsiders," and "the [group] began reflecting this in its own thinking." Accordingly, a member tried to find Negroes who would pass out applications for the group at a mass meeting of Negroes. He wanted to "make it less identifiable." A White member of a predominantly Negro civil rights group tried to find Negroes who would offer his resolutions at staff meetings. He wanted to "avoid a racial conflict."

The process can also be charted as the exemptive categories become increasingly constricted. It is the more experienced Whites who use constrictions. Their experience necessitates this approach, but it also occasionally provides a defense that is unavailable to others. For White civil rights workers usually find, as one realized in retrospect, that "it was easier to criticize the other Whites" than oneself. But it is generally just those with sufficient experience who can use this facility as a defense, because it is easiest for them to agree with the condemnation of White workers while exempting themselves. Another White was able to retrospectively describe the thinking of those who put themselves beyond the reach of criticism: "They couldn't be talking about me; they mean the inexperienced, irresponsible volunteers" (in the process, whatever capacity for indignation still remains is now directed against the neophyte White).

Through progressively expanded concessions, resulting from progressively constricted categories, the White advances to the next stage. A White, who had just heard the Negro members of a civil rights organization damn White activists, suggested the Negroes were "against the White man for perpetuating the system, not the White man himself." Another White, who was a reporter for a newspaper started by civil rights workers, found herself condemned by Negroes because its contents were "projecting everything we're fighting." In defending herself, she went beyond the preceding distinction between the guilty act and the innocent actor. The distinction arose between the guilty past and innocent present of the actor: "Maybe it's because of the White background we come from." Although the act was committed during the present, she could salvage her innocence so long as the "background" is not a foreground and is what she has "come from" rather than is operating in.

The progression of the White is assisted by his continually presenting what he considers to be the ultimate argument, and the Negro showing it is the penultimate. The exchange is not usually so formal as this suggests, but it was on one occasion when a teacher, who had just heard an argument against White participation in the Movement, conceded the guilt of his foreground: "Recognizing the attitudes I bring as a White, don't I also bring some attitudes that outweigh them? I found some people who have been debauched by religion. I try to liberate my students from this kind of bondage and other kinds of bondage . . . developing a sense of what's in your own mind." The Negro answered: "I think those attitudes may be valid. But I think if those attitudes are valid, they'll come out as people progress in what they think and express. . . . They themselves have to discover. The discovery to them is more important. It gives them a sense of dignity, a sense of power. It makes them a whole person." On another occasion, a Negro student was more explicit about the invalidity of "valid" attitudes or acts. As a reason for why "There shouldn't be any White faculty at ———," he noted, "If you want anything to be done, you know who you have to go to." His reference here is to the frequency with which White faculty aid the students in their grievances against the administration and participate in civil rights demonstrations, while the Negro faculty do neither. The contrast gives the other students a further reason for believing that, as he says, "right is White."

As the White runs out of distinctions (there are few available after separating the present from the present, as in the last case), he moves toward the final plateau of recognition. But the fall is still considerable, and the eventual shock is not so much absorbed as delayed. Insofar as it does not succeed as a defense, this process succeeds as a transition to the next stage.

chapter four

DISMAY

A positive way to say the White of the preceding stage is trying to demonstrate his exemption from Whiteness or mistrust, is that he is trying to demonstrate his inclusion in Blackness or trust. As the White progresses through the stages of awareness, conversion serves as more than a means of persuading himself that he belongs; he also sees it as necessary for persuading the Negro that he belongs. The acquisition of Blackness appears as the only basis on which trust can be established. But it is not until the present stage that a variety of converging and convincing factors compel the White to recognize the impossibility of conversion, and therefore of trust.

VULNERABILITY OF CONVERSION-CLAIMANTS

Once the difficulties of conversion are recognized, they are conclusive, because there is no appeal. The White finds himself as exposed as he had once been shielded. The closely related components of this defenselessness include the following:

1. Before reaching this stage, the White agrees that the Negro is entitled to self-determination. The agreement is unqualified because he assumed their determination will be one that is acceptable to him. When, on reaching this stage, he discovers that it leaves no room for his presence, he cannot protest without denying the right of self-determination. A White who found the nationalism in a civil rights organization made his participation untenable also felt that "I have no right to say" what the objectives of nationalism ought to be.

2. In addition to supporting the right of the Negro to make his own evaluations, the White agrees, in varying degrees, with the evaluations themselves. They are the same ones that had fortified his commitment to the Movement, while self-exemption was possible. "They're right; they're 100 percent right. If they were wrong I would fight it . . . I would say they were crazy. And if I admit they're right, it's like holding a shovel and digging my own grave."

3. The Negro has the authority for defining the accusation. There is no way of contradicting his estimate of how a White is regarded by a Negro. "They called me a 'missionary'; and I used to call a lot of people 'missionary.'"

4. Through a personal involvement, any defense against the accusation gives an appearance of defending oneself, rather than a principle. The result is a fear that credulity is reduced. "Because of my obvious vested interest, I can't do anything positive [by way of self-defense]."

5. In referring to a White who was planning to leave a civil rights organization because the racial mistrust against him had become unmistakable, another White said: "He can't defend himself strategically or emotionally." The White tries to defend himself against Negroes ("strategically") and himself ("emotionally"). Insofar as they can be separated, the emotional component is unavoidably more salient; being personal, it is more compelling. The focus on it deflects from the strategic effort. Briefly, (4) is concerned with the way a "vested interest" affects others, while (5) is concerned with the way "vested interest" affects oneself.

6. The emotional response of the White is defensive; for an offense, he relies on logical appeals. But the response of the Negro to the White is also emotional. He is therefore impervious to such dispassionate approaches. A White civil rights worker had what he called a "stock question" when confronted with mistrust. After naming a conservative Negro businessman and a radical White activist, he asked hostile

Negroes which they would prefer as a source of "leadership
or advice." Invariably, they "ignored it."

7. By defending himself against charges, the White
finds himself in the same relation to Negroes as those Whites
whom he had considered the proper enemies. At staff meetings of a civil rights organization, a White sounded to himself
like "the red neck who assures integrationists that 'We
haven't done anything to you' before he beats you over the
head."

The defenselessness of the White is furthered by the
defenselessness of the Negro who might seek contact with
him. To begin with, it is difficult for the Negro to provide a
defense against himself. He is sometimes able to find Whites
with whom he can, on one level, have a personal rather than
a racial relationship. But on another level he sees himself
trafficking with the White enemy. Because of this betrayal,
he himself becomes the enemy. One Negro civil rights worker
stated, "I hate myself for hating Albin, because he's a friend;
and I hate Albin for liking me, because he's White."

This objectification of himself is, in its own right, a betrayal. It is a negation of Negroness, since the greatest com-
pliment one Negro can pay another, or himself, is that he is
"together." (In all likelihood, the term arose with reference
to Negroes who asserted themselves in the presence of
Whites, and thereby reversed the traditional behavior that a
Negro civil rights worker described in a report: "The Negro
in the black belt of Alabama has always had to leave some of
himself outside when talking to Whites. . . .") This quintes-
sence of Negroness is sacrificed by objectification—which requires a splintering of the self.

Throughout the relationship, his old racial feelings are
in counterpoint with the new nonracial ones, and dominate.
The marriage of Albin (as he has been renamed here) to a
Negro could be considered either the ultimate racial or nonracial act; he reacted as a Negro: "I resented it when he

married a colored girl . . . like in the city, when you move in on my turf."

These divided feelings express themselves in divided actions. A White student at a Negro college was approached by another student who hit him repeatedly in the stomach while calling him "White boy," and concluded by telling an onlooker that this is "one of the few White folks I like." Another Negro member of the group who calls him "White boy" explains its divided significance:

> [He] gets called "White boy" as a term of almost affection, because the same kids who call him "White boy" will say to someone else who does: "That ain't no White boy, that's a nigger;" and [the White] will laugh. It's also to put him in his place though; because he tries to act Negro very often, especially through his speech patterns, and you call him that to say: "You're not that hip. You're White; so stop trying. You'll never make it to a Black degree of toughness."

The ambivalence of the Negro gradually causes Whites to view their situation in terms that are equally divided (and, again, not divided equally). "If we're going somewhere in the car," a White civil rights worker related that the Negroes "might say 'Get in the back, hunky,' or something silly like that." When asked about it being "silly," she stated that "We've got past it in [terms of] human relationships"; but, at the same time, "It'll always be there." Although testing and acceptance are, at best, mutually exclusive, the "White boy" concluded, "After you're accepted, you're still tested."

Even if it were possible for the White to win over individual Negroes, little would be accomplished. A White can only undergo a successful conversion when the entire Negro community with which he is dealing has been convinced of his conversion. The Uncle Tom label, applied by unconvinced members of the community, would foreclose both a defense and further contact with the White. It proclaims the designee to have probably engaged in a trust relationship with the White man, and as a result, to have certainly violated his trust relationship with Negroes. Once the relationship, however instrumental it may be, crosses sexual as well as racial lines, the offender has sinned; other Negroes impale him on a transplanted religious term—he is a "backslider."

At the same time, an individual White is unlikely to be accepted so long as other Whites are rejected as a category. For the standardized way in which Whites are appraised draws all of its assumptions and conclusions from the untrustworthiness of all Whites. It is likely to be as disconcerting for a Negro to find a trustworthy White, as it is for a White to find an untrusting Negro. In either case, the entire framework would collapse, with a resultant disorientation.

The reciprocal is that all Whites must be able to accept Negroes. It is not enough for an individual White to be capable of accepting Negroes, while other Whites are incapable of doing so. In fact, it appears to the Negro as mutually exclusive. The contradiction within complete acceptance by an incomplete population of Whites was expressed by a student who insisted she "could never trust any White." For if he did not "hold back" information from his classes in an effort to "keep them down," he would eventually be forced to because "other Whites would resent him; he wouldn't be a member of the race."

Further, just as there are penalties for having less mistrust than most other Negroes, there are rewards for having more—or at least expressing it more effectively. As one Negro said about those in a campus civil rights organization who were more blatantly mistrustful of Whites: "It makes kids feel that you perhaps didn't just happen into the Movement, but that you've always been your own movement." The Negro cannot act beyond the call of duty, since his duty, where racial, can advance indefinitely; yet, he can have a duty that appears to be beyond the call heard by other Negroes.

The White is also hampered by the fact that prospective converts feel obligated to purge themselves of their past. They are, in effect, trying to be reborn as Negroes. However much the White wants to forsake his past, he begins to discover that the past is not always as anxious to forsake him.

One of the most persistent forms taken by the past is prejudice. Probably no White is free of vestigial prejudice, that is, the prejudice originating at some point before his engagement in the Movement. It is usually well hidden from the White himself. The process of discovering one is unaccepting is closely related to discovering one is unaccepted. In both cases, the discovery usually depends on some form of encounter with the Negro. The following account, by a student, describes the encounter that provided a White instructor with his first glimpse into the thinking of the Negro and, as a result, himself:

> I talked with [the White instructor] for about four hours. Right after we began talking he said that he'd like to ask me something. He then told of how he'd been sitting in the Union with [a Negro instructor] when a student came up to her and told of a series of meetings that he expected to see her at: about student-White teacher relationships, and of the resentment between the two groups. He said he was sort of overlooked by the student, he remarked that maybe this was because the student didn't know him. After I admitted I knew nothing of it, we discussed what it might be. I told him of instances last year where the students felt the White instructors were trying to govern [the student civil rights organization]. He then went

on to say in a heated manner that "If they're going to have a lot of shit like this going on, I'll leave. I'd planned to stay, but I didn't come here to get involved in a lot of crap like that. If that's the type of thing that'll be going on, I'll go." He said: "I know there's a certain amount of uneasiness and discomfort in all Black-White relationships, even like now with me and you. When I first came here, I noticed and felt that I was before Black faces, but as time wore on they ceased to be Black faces, and became just faces of students. Since I could stop seeing Black, I can conceive that the students can stop seeing White, and I think they do. I can't notice anything of the sort in my class." I kidded him about whether he ever said to himself, "Damn niggers are dumb." He said yes, he did make little jokes like that to himself.

Specifically, it is his initial exposure to both the unacceptance and the unaccepting. In each case, his response is preliminary. He is no more than indignant about learning he is unaccepted; he sees no grounds for it, least of all in himself. At this stage, his limited accepting is approached tentatively by both him and the student. She is able to elicit his acknowledgement of it only by pretending it is nothing more than a "joke."

The Negro is able to see the prejudice of Whites from a vantage point that is unavailable to the White. Even as no more than an attitude, the crystallization of prejudice is only possible when a target has been found. In an important sense, the target is closer to the prejudice than the White.

At the same time, it is difficult for anyone to acknowledge his prejudice, because prejudice is itself a prejudicial term. But the prejudiced individual is usually spared this self-recognition, since underlying his prejudice is the belief that his views are grounded in truth. The Movement White, however, cannot share this belief in the truthfulness of views that run counter to the premises of the Movement. While these premises might otherwise free him to see his prejudice clearly, they also make the prejudicial implications of his prejudice more costly, so that the net effect is astigmatism.

The resultant capacity of the Negro, and incapacity of the White, to recognize prejudice in the White could be seen at a civil rights office when Whites entering for the first time sought information from a White, who was seated there, rather than a Negro.[1] The Negro, who was ignored while also sitting in the office, commented, "They only showed me respect when they were told I was someone they were supposed to respect," for he was in charge of the office.

He believed, "You can't find no White woman anywhere who'll work for a Negro—ironing his clothes all day, and leave pleasantly." This illustrated his feeling that all Whites were unable to work for Negroes, "They've got a block." His generalizations about the way Whites generalize served as an introduction for the following account of how he and a White civil rights worker had driven to a new assignment together, as contrasted to their arrival:

> We had a great drive over here. We stayed at my girl's and had breakfast there, we stopped and had ice cream . . . and then we went to [a restaurant at their destination] for a cup of coffee. I said "We should approach [the local Negro attorney whose political campaign they were supposed to help organize] with something written down." I asked him what he wanted to do [during the campaign]. He said "He probably already has something written down for us." I said to myself: "I'll be goddamned; he doesn't want to work under me because I'm a Negro."

[1] The usual distinction between prejudice and discrimination has little meaning in the context discussed here. The Negro, and ultimately the White, is primarily concerned with what these acts reveal—and that is prejudice. Also, these acts do not always reveal discrimination in the usual sense.

(This version was presented with the White present. The
Negro later wrote an essay for his own use about the incident, entitled "The Inevitable Superiorist (sic) of the White
Worker," in which the last "he" that appears in the above
account read "the cracker.") The Negro had been placed in
charge of this project by the national office, but he felt the
attorney was being used against him, as a "lever," by the
White so "He [the attorney] would be over us equally." The
White vehemently denied this interpretation. However, later
that day, after he reported having "a chance to think about
it," and without the Negro present, the White conceded its
truth. The Negro had said about himself and the White: "We
drink together, we talk about our girls; but he can't accept
the idea of working under a Negro." The White now decided
that he and the Negro "are great buddies . . . until it comes
to working together." One of the specifics granted was that
"he's right: unconsciously I was using [the attorney] as a
'lever' against him."

    While exempting himself from prejudice, he employed
the techniques familiar to mistrust exemption, such as neutral categories and equivalence. The Negro cited an instance
when the White had spoken angrily to the attorney. At the
time it was mentioned, the White attributed it to "contemp-
tuousness," which "I have toward a lot of people—including
Whites"; he further noted that the attorney had it towards
others of his race. But he also decided later that, on the contrary, "It was racial." The defenses of the White were eventually made inoperative by the revelations. His view of himself was thoroughly dislocated. After acknowledging the
Negro had been accurate, he went on to recognize that "deep
down inside, I see the Negro in the Movement as a Black
Sambo . . . as a young Uncle Remus. I realized it all of a
sudden." He now saw more of what he thought to be his
prejudice than the Negro did.

    These confrontations are scarce. Whites usually go

through a period of believing that the precise grounds for the resistance they encounter should "be brought into the open," as one expressed it. Their hope is that it will result in improved contacts with Negroes, who, however, have little interest in this precision, because they have no interest in an improvement within the existing context.

The confrontation described above led to one obstruction being replaced by another. After hearing the charges, the White told a third party that "I'm going to make an overt effort to make things go more smoothly . . . I'm going to be more tactful." When his new policy was underway, the White reported, "I feel more comfortable: things are more defined." He considered it to be reciprocal, since his Negro colleague "is much happier working with me." But the Negro did not consider himself happier; instead he complained to the third party that the White was continually asking himself: "'Am I challenging him because he's a Negro?' He's frozen."

When, unlike this confrontation, Whites themselves initiate their discovery of prejudice, it is usually by inadvertence; for the prejudice, in this situation, appears openly and reflexively. A recognition of it is forced on the White since there is no time to erect the defenses that normally obscure its nature—at least from himself. When a White exchange student, visiting the home of a Negro family, was offered his choice of two cigarette brands, he replied: "I can't tell one Negro from another." He was no less astonished than his hosts; as he commented much later, "I don't know how that came out." Together with discovering what he believes is prejudice, the White discovers how little control he has over his dealings with himself, to say nothing of the Negro.

The fraility of their past is accentuated for the Whites who eventually discover it by their idealization of the Negro. As idealized, the Negro is still subjected to prejudice, for he is seen according to a preconceived judgement, and therefore, as one of a group rather than as one. The difference between these prejudices expresses itself in the adjective most often used by White civil rights workers to describe the attributes or artifacts of the Negro: "beautiful." The term conveys a sense of flawlessness. A White civil rights worker presented his deliberate picture of Negroes through a poem about one he had met in Birmingham; it concluded: "And when they beat you/ I will bleed/ For I am followin'/ Where you lead." Yet, when he thought of Negroes he also found himself inadvertently thinking of his wallet, and his hand inadvertently moved to his back pocket to make certain it had not been stolen. The contrast between past and present is further heightened by the elevation of their Cause. On the one hand, a civil rights organization, comprised mainly of Whites, had a list of objectives that began with "Accomplishment of a completely integrated society," and closed with "An end to man's inhumanity to man." On the other hand, the organization was represented at a conference by a staff member who, one evening there, heard the screams of a girl, and his "immediate reaction was that one of the Negroes was raping the shit out of her."

Whites are all the more troubled by their racial atavism because they usually have no idea that other Whites harbor the same sort of feelings. One civil rights worker stated: "I want to make a confession. Here I am a White girl; I've heard a lot of crap about Negroes from my friends, and I've always fought it. But I've been afraid to admit prejudice. Something I say will be judged wrongly—not necessarily by my Negro friends, but maybe by White radicals." For these Whites are often more outraged than the Negro upon detecting prejudice in another White.

The White has ordinarily developed his view of the Negro in isolation from him. This view probably first appeared before the White cared whether it was acceptable to the Negro. Later, on the eve of joining the Movement, when he did care (or even if he cared all along), there was not likely to have been much opportunity for testing the acceptability of his view. The only criterion for nonprejudice that is available before joining the Movement is unacceptable to the White. For his romanticization of the Negro is incompatible with gauging his behavior by the dictum that was typically expressed as "How superficial these [racial] differences really are." (This particular version appeared in the guide to a conference dealing with "Human Relations"—a term that in itself expressed this position, since it is a substitute for "Race Relations.")

Therefore, to the White who has been made aware of his prejudice, nonprejudice is a *terra incognita*. A White teacher noted the high proportion in his classes of female students with "the cutest asses." He then quickly asked his only listener, a White colleague, "Is that prejudice?" His concern was not whether this observation was unbefitting a teacher, but whether it was unbefitting a White.

Again, there is a need for guidelines and none are considered appropriate. The result is paralysis. His sudden preoccupation with prejudice means the White chronically dreads, as mentioned by a teacher, "offending people [i.e., Negroes]"; this requires a condition that he summarizes as "being ready." He demonstrated the dread on one occasion by interrupting a new White teacher who had begun to comment "But the Negro. . . ." The interruption was accompanied by a warning: "Be discreet!" There were Negroes in the vicinity, so the new White waited until they returned to their office to ask, as he later recalled, "What did I do? What did I say?" The other White was discreet about his own discretion: "I thought you said 'Those people.'" His apprehension follows from the fact that, in almost every case, when the Negro offends the White, it is by saying the White has offended the Negro.

Yet, this apprehension is so removed from his prior

experience that it is not immediately sensed by the Negro dealing with Movement Whites for the first time. Upon finding it, the Negro shifts his behavior toward these Whites. But the transition does not mean the Negro considers the Movement White to be basically different from the traditional White; it does mean the Negro realizes the Movement White considers himself to be basically different.

Freshmen, during their first semester, are among those Negroes who have not yet undergone the transition. As one said, "First you think: 'Is he prejudiced: Is he going to flunk me because I'm a Negro?'" Any teaching procedure of the White is viewed as evidence of the same prejudice. At one extreme, "My instructor thought that the class was dumb, and consequently he taught at a very slow pace." At the other, a student suggested that whenever White teachers "go too fast," it is because they believe "we can't learn anything."

During this period, the students work in a way intended to overcome the stereotype; in the process they reverse the procedure used for dealing with the Southern White. Traditionally, it has been to the advantage of Southern Negroes to indulge the stereotypes held by Whites. If employers—for instance, those encountered by the students during their summer jobs—believed the Negro was not an effective worker, he could work ineffectively with impunity. Nothing was gained by trying to prove himself effective, since there was a ceiling on advancement, and the possibility of being labeled a "smart nigger." But in the classroom it initially appears to him that transcending stereotypes will be necessary for a suitable grade. Therefore, the students, according to one of them, "work more for Whites . . . they want to prove to them that they're really not ignorant as they think."

By the beginning of the second semester, however, the students have discovered that the White teachers are trying to prove themselves. Their discovery is based on contact with the teacher, as well as with upperclassmen and Negro faculty members. As one experienced student told others, "They are sympathizers. [Laughter.] They have guilty feelings about the way the Negro has been treated by the Whites, and they are trying to compensate for their wrongdoings." Another student observed that White teachers try to "show they're not like the other Whites around here [the South]." One way of showing their dissimilarity is to reduce the number of failures by basing grades on a curve, whether through the use of statistics, or through simply lowering their expectations. The result is a system much like the one traditionally used by Southern Whites, where a lower standard is applied to Negroes in all areas of life, as exemplified by reduced criteria for Negro doctors being licensed.

The discovery of the students does not require them to abandon their stereotype of the White's stereotype; instead they find new ways of making it relevant. The focus simply shifts to aspects of the stereotype that accord with discovering the White is on the defensive. A student observed the White faculty "seem frightened of us. One of my teachers was frightened to death. Well, I guess she had a right to, since she has heard so many stories about how violent we Negroes are." In all respects, the inner response of the Negro does not distinguish between the White teacher and the traditional White after the discovery: "White instructors were a new experience for me; and after two years here, I still haven't gotten used to them. I don't trust them, and I have a feeling of contempt for them. I guess it's the way they've treated us. They're here trying to take over, as they have done everywhere else." Others have been more specific about the emotional continuity: White teachers "ask questions that seem embarrassing"; for example, whether the class discussing *Huckleberry Finn* thought "Tom was using Jim."

After discovering the White teachers are trying to prove themselves, students stop trying to prove themselves. This means a substantial decrease in the amount of homework that they do. The burden is shifted to the teacher. It is now known that so far from failing students because they are Negroes, the teacher will pass them for this reason. One White told a colleague, "I don't feel that I have the right to flunk a student . . . I'd feel guilty about it."

The decrease in academic work is accompanied by an increase in nonacademic work that has the same objective of securing a favorable grade (otherwise, the student can be sure of not failing, but not of an A). For the students soon develop ways of using prejudice attributed to Whites as a lever. In the first place, this prejudice becomes a reminder to the Negro that each is in a separate world. The Negro is then reminded that to the extent these worlds are apart, he can safely manipulate the White; beginning with slavery, this fact has been proven to the satisfaction of the Negro (and documented for others through the publication of slave narratives). The White on the campus, as on the plantation, is often unable and always unwilling to recognize when he is being manipulated—or, as the students call it, "sanded." The derivative significance of this term has alternatively been seen by students as "putting sand in their eyes" and "wearing them down"; either way, it represents disarming the opposition. Although both races are sanded, the remoteness of the White gives this activity a racial significance. One student determined, "White teachers are easier [to sand], because they don't understand us like the Negro teachers."

Students further decide that the historic technique of manipulating Whites will result in "heavy sand" if it is given an altogether new content. Instead of the traditional understated interest in civil rights, it is now necessary to overstate this interest. As "a fine example of sanding," a student described what happened when one of her classmates took a course from a White instructor during the second semester of his freshman year: "He became an active member of the campus civil rights activities, which the instructor is an active member in." Similarly, instead of understating an interest in White women, it is considered helpful to overstate such an interest, since it is believed that "Male students can sand better to White female instructors; White women are known to like our men."

The historic rationale for manipulating Whites, retribution, is also present. Through what is considered prejudice, the White provides the Negro with a justification, as well as an opportunity, for improving his position. A student insisted she would "definitely sand White teachers" in preference to Negroes; for the obverse of their prejudice toward the "dumb" student is that "They think they're so smart." She concludes, "They've taken advantage of me, so now I'll get even." Moreover, the White teacher is seen as trying to sand the students. For sanding is, essentially, the means of making an artificial trust relationship look authentic to the other party. A White teacher, who left the classroom while an examination was underway, caused one of his students to suppose that even what he acknowledged as "trust" on the part of the instructor, was not what it appeared to be: "White teachers use trust as a tool. He wanted to use trust to get in deeper with them [the students] . . . I figure he had some other reason than trust in his heart." Another observed that although White instructors are trying to sand the students, "they do a very bad job of it" because "they try to persuade the students that they're for Negroes" by means of a contrived dedication (that the students meet with a contrived dedication): "[the White faculty] try to show a great deal of interest in civil rights."

Prejudice primarily acts to the advantage of the Negro insofar as the White goes out of his way to prove it is nonexistent. Before arriving at this inverted prejudice, however, the White must determine the extent of his initial prejudice. Since he is usually unable to recognize the prejudice by himself, he relies on the Negro to assay it. The Negro, in turn, is able to find evidence of prejudice wherever he is seeking the benefits of its inversion. Whether the Negro is trying to borrow a car or seduce a woman, if the White is reluctant the reason is prejudice: "You don't want to because I'm a Negro." The vulnerability of the White to charges of prejudice offers the Negro unlimited opportunities. Any lack of accommodation can become the basis for a stereotype of Whites which, the Negro knows, is regarded by the White as no less in need of inversion than a stereotype he holds of the Negro. When a White hesitated to drive a Negro civil rights worker to a distant tavern, he was told that "White folks just don't like to go clubbing."

Objectively harmless stereotypes, for instance an aversion to "clubbing," work as well as any. For the Negro implies, and the White assumes, that no stereotype of the White is discrete. Instead, it is thought to operate as one stereotype within an interconnected constellation of them. Confirmation of an objectively harmless one is, therefore, considered tantamount to confirming an objectively damaging one. Efforts to disprove the one are no less vigorous than efforts to disprove the other.

Throughout, the Negro is trying to discover what if any limits exist on the extent to which the White will invert his prejudice. A White teacher was walking near his campus when a car full of high-school-aged Negroes stopped, and one of the passengers said: "Hey, would you loan me a dollar?" The teacher refused, since they thought "I was a White do-gooder." His interpretation resulted from never having seen the students before; he could afford to make it because he never expected to see them again. The situation was altered for him when students in his class requested loans. But it was not altered for the Negro observer—for instance, the chairman of his department who discouraged him from complying when he was on the verge of doing so. While contrasting this teacher and another who gave equally difficult exams, a student noted that "only those people who really studied" and did poorly would see the Negro teacher after class, whereas "anyone would go up to [the White teacher]." Moreover, "They try to push [the White teacher]; they wouldn't try to push [the Negro teacher]." Pushing becomes a highly developed technique, for as another student remarked about his classmates, "They have to find out how far a [White] teacher will let them go."

In the process, the Negro does provide the White with guidelines, although compliance with them multiplies his unacceptability, since it is considered by Negroes to underscore his unacceptance of them. Movement Whites are, according to a Negro civil rights worker, "too afraid to refuse."

As the White continues on his own the alertness to prejudice, a further problem arises. When the White is oversensitive to his own prejudice, he attracts the attention of Negroes no less than when he is undersensitive. The result of seeing a Whiteness signal that the Negro had not noticed can be equal to ignoring one the Negro saw. The following was observed by a Negro student during a discussion group:

> As [a Negro instructor] gave the background history of Rhodesia, she mentioned the fact that the first White men arrived in the 1650's. She asked [a White instructor from South Africa] to affirm this date. He did so, but seemed rather shy with the mentioning of the word "White." A Negro boy noticed this shyness and began to smile. All the people's eyes were glued on [the Negro instructor] as she talked. Only [the White instructor] was busy doing other things. He played with his tie, rubbed his nose, crossed and uncrossed his legs, scratched his face with his gloves, pounded on the arm of his chair, and showed other signs of seeming

anxiety. As she talked about the Whites in Africa, he looked out of place. His presence seemed all wrong to me!

In fact, when circumspection appears to surround prejudice, it tends to provoke mistrust more readily than forthright prejudice by raising the question of where else deception is at work in the relationship.

Unaccepting and nonacceptance are resisted and discovered by a similar process because they have a similar meaning for the White. Most basically, they both represent barriers to a trust relationship. The disclosure of prejudice contributes to a feeling of self-mistrust. The reasons behind this self-mistrust include some of those that result in the mistrust of Whites by Negroes; for instance, the White learning he has little control over his own acts, just as the Negro feels he cannot protect himself from those acts. Although this self-mistrust thereby provides the White with a form of empathy that was previously unattainable, it diminishes his feeling of being totally qualified for a trust relationship.

The self-mistrust is increased by the activities intended to refute prejudice. Whereas the Negro believes he knows the reason behind these activities, the White suspects, but his suspicion has the same effect as confirmation. For any doubt beclouds and, consequently, vitiates the act. Moreover, this doubt shifts to other activities, just as the Negro shifts his certitude, regardless of whether the first or subsequent acts originated as a refutation. When a White girl tried to form a relationship, she asked herself: "Am I with him because he's a Negro?" The question was persistent and self-sufficient. It, rather than an answer to it, finally precluded a relationship for her.

In some respects, prejudice and mistrust are distinct. For instance, prejudice denotes an inadequate basis for its preconception; while mistrust is neutral in this regard—the preconception from which it arises may or may not be in-adequate. (The principal means used for identifying preju-dice here has been whether the initiator and/or target of the viewpoint regarded it as such.) But a connection between the two terms appears when the White begins to lose his de-fenses; he is then likely to discover what he considers his mis-trust for the Negro, in addition to prejudice. A White who had been forced to evacuate his fortress found himself real-izing for the first time that "I don't have much trust for the Negro—not only about stealing, but about competency." At this point of self-awareness, the White achieves a symmetry in his relationship with the Negro, but instead of being based on trust, it is based on mistrust.

NEGROES ASSISTED BY WHITES OBSTRUCT THE CONVERSION

There is an asymmetry to the form of symmetry that the White wants the Negro to acknowledge, as opposed to the kind he does acknowledge. While the Negro is willing to acknowledge that the White also mistrusts, he will not ac-knowledge that the White can "think Black." A White claimed this ability in an article written for the newsletter of a civil rights organization, where he began by explaining that:

> It is hard for someone who has not lived in ———— these past months and in the Negro community of that small town in the southwest corner of Mississippi to understand the reality behind the two bombings of ————. The following account is written to convey some of that reality.

This introduction provides one of the few successful ways (for the White, at any rate) to deal with the problem of pro-nouns that often faces the White. A White student at a Negro college reported, "I hate to use 'we' and 'they'; it's what we're fighting against. I use it only when I'm forced to." A White instructor on a committee dealing with problems in the Negro community "didn't feel right saying 'We need' and 'They need,'" so he resigned. But by trying "to convey some of that reality," the White activist establishes a pretext for using the first person, as appears in the following sections from the same article:

> And then the moments of torment that follow [the sound of the explosion]—whose house, who is dead? It's not mine. Then who? My neighbor, my brother, my son. . . . Who? and one's stomach aches with pain and the pain seeps up into the chest and the head and comes out of every paw [sic]. . . . Here comes the police. The same police who have beaten our fathers and raped our daughters—and put our children in jail.

A later incident, involving the same White, emphasized how unwilling Negroes on the staff were to accept his capacity to see the world through the eyes, or even the glasses, of a Negro. One of these Negroes wrote the following narrative about attempts to establish a newspaper for the Negro community in which the national office of the organization was located:

> [White staff members] were present in the meetings where we discussed purpose and name for the newspaper. The people who were against the name "Nitty Gritty" were primarily [Whites]. . . . The truth, the torch, etc. were suggested by those opposing the name "Nitty Gritty." Things like this caused many of us to wonder if these people would be able to work on a paper that has the aims that the Black members of the project had in mind. From then on, things became more tense in the meetings. A move made on the Black people's part to insure the Blackness of the paper was that all articles must be reviewed by the entire staff,

and that all project persons would vote on the ultimate layout.

One day, [a Negro], who had been chosen as the project director, and I went into the back meeting room at _____ and found [the Whites] in a meeting planning the first edition of the "Nitty Gritty." Some articles had been written, completely in a vacuum from the community. . . . The black members of the project decided that we had to do something to insure that the aims of the paper were carried out, i.e., the projection of Blackness, and the necessity for solodarity [sic] between Black people in this country and Black people in Africa and Asia, as well as citing who the real enemy is, white society. We knew that this meant getting an aware Black editor and Black writers for the Newspaper.

Although Negroes become Black by responding to Whites, Whites try to become Black by responding to Negroes. Much that the Negro borrowed from the White has been used, often out of necessity, in private. Therefore, the Negro could practice his use of the borrowings with a minimum of exposure to the ridicule or antagonism of the willing or unwilling lenders. But another result of this privacy was that the borrowings underwent a certain amount of rearrangement, for there was no way of using them in their precisely original contexts. The White seeking conversion must, then, attempt to borrow back these rearrangements that are all the more difficult to master because they are so like his own culture; it is only the nuances that make them distinguishable. Moreover, he tries to reclaim and incorporate them in full view of the Negro.

Whites are equally disadvantaged whether or not they can imitate the Negro accurately. On the one hand, they are confronted by the obverse of stereotypes originated by

Whites. At an off-campus party, students laughed while a teacher tried to dance the Boston Monkey because, as one explained afterwards, "White folks can't dance." On the other hand, a White civil rights worker, who discovered that an accurate imitation has its own dangers, decided against joining Negroes in a dance, because, "It would be worse if I could do it than if I couldn't. . . . The people needed to prove they can do something Whites can't."

Another underlying difficulty arises because superordination and subordination affect the holders of these positions in ways that are as dissimilar as they are relevant to the problem of conversion. In the one case, superordination is relevant to the extent those occupying the position are unaffected by it. Usually, those who dominate have little self-consciousness about their position, or awareness of the dominated, because there has been no need for defending themselves and otherwise adjusting to external requirements. This adjustment can easily become a way of life for the subordinate group that resists the superordinate group. To carry out the defiance with impunity demands a constant sensitivity to those who are in a position to punish the violators. One technique for operating with impunity is to reassure the superordinate group that it has no need for concern with self or others. Furthermore, the superordinate group locates itself in what it considers the natural order of things, so that the sheer fact of its superordination is proof of its rightness.

This isolation continues by means of learning Blackness from the Negro, since the White is not dealing with its reason for being. There are few peculiarly Negro, or originally Negro, cultural characteristics that were not intended to mitigate the dominance by Whites. The term "Man" is a simple, but representative, case. Negroes use it at the same junctures in conversation among themselves as Whites use "Boy" in addressing them. Instead of undergoing Blackness,

Whites are acquiring it second-hand,[2] which partly accounts for their ability to romanticize the world of the Negro.[3]

However, what turns out to be the most persuasive obstruction to conversion is that the longer the White remains in the Movement, the more he learns to think like a Negro. For learning to think like a Negro does not result in conversion to Blackness. On the contrary, it reveals to the White the unattainability of this conversion. He learns not so much about Blackness as he does about Whiteness.

Most of the insights that the White has into the outlook of the Negro result from sounding the alarm of Whiteness. His dependence on the Negro for a correct assessment of his Whiteness is illustrated by the contrast between the following two cases. A White trying to organize Negroes in a Southern city encountered a Negro woman who had broken her leg by falling through a hole in her house. The landlord, after the White asked "what he was going to do about it," sent her a piece of quarter-inch plywood to repair the floor. By way of trying to provoke her into protest, the White said the landlord, also White, "treats you like a rat."

[2] This rule is proved by the exception of John Howard Griffin. As described in *Black Like Me*, he visibly became a Negro in order to answer: "What is it like to experience discrimination based on skin color, something over which one has no control?" [Boston, Houghton Mifflin, 1961, p. 1.] His narrative shows that contrary to his intentions and awareness, he continually exercised "control." For he revealed his original color to Negroes; he reassured himself it was a masquerade; he periodically escaped to live among Whites as a White; and finally he returned permanently to his life as a White—a prospect that was always present.

[3] In the same way, those Blacks, whether Negroes or Africans, who most romanticize Blackness have been furthest removed from the constraints of subjugation. The most notable example of this simultaneous freedom from place and elevation of Blackness has been Léopold Senghor who composed, on the one hand the French Constitution, and on the other Négritude poetry. In a disproportionate number of cases, Black nationalist leaders in the United States have, like Senghor, been married to White women, or otherwise involved with them. The alliance means, as one Negro husband expressed it, "I had to fight harder to prove I hadn't deserted the race." Whereas, the Negro tends to assume he provides enough proof to be able to afford the alliance when he has already established himself as an advocate of Black narcissism.

She replied, "I was born a rat." The White would-be organizer said nothing further: "I was stopped; she had psychologically abdicated." A Negro activist from the same city who heard him recounting the exchange was asked, without the White present, whether he felt the woman actually believed her own remark. He stated, "Definitely not, she was waiting for him to say something else; [so she could discover:] 'Am I being made a fool? Nobody bothered all along—why now?' "
In another Southern city, a White working with several Negro youths was able to reflect their thinking more accurately because their thinking was, presumably, reflected more accurately in their statements to him. On one occasion he tried to explain to them the reason for their anger at a Confederate flag encountered on a car. In describing the incident, he said "I felt like a hypocrite; as though I'd been through it myself." When asked whether the Negroes had responded to his explanation, he cited their rhetorical questions: "How do you know; did you paint yourself White?" and "How do you know; did you turn yourself inside out?"

The White, in time, is able to respond to his Whiteness with the same intensity as the Negro. As this intensity becomes similar, the nature of the response becomes dissimilar. A White, who was considered typical of many working in the South at the time, was followed by photographers in preparation for an article about her in a national magazine. Negroes on the staff of the civil rights organization that was supervising her work complained the article should be about a local Negro. Another White, who had considerable experience in the Movement and was aware of these complaints, later found himself featured in a church magazine. He says: "I felt pangs of guilt. . . . It should've been one of the local people." In contrast to the aggressive responses of the Negro, the White undergoes passive responses—such as guilt.

Where there is an excess of anticipating Negroes' responses, it works against the involvement that is necessary for effective anticipation. Excessive anticipation easily produces a self-consciousness that was noticed by a student who commented that the White teacher "tries to watch himself too carefully, and then he stumbles." Similarly, learning to anticipate responses of the Negro requires an involvement with him that is contradictory to the anticipation. At the point of emersing himself in contacts with the Negro, the White must remember the necessity of being an observer as well as a participant. The problem was encountered by a Southern White at a Negro college: "I'm very careful to say 'knee-grow'. . . . I've caught myself, without thinking [about to say 'nigger']. It's so easy to use it the way they do."

The White is accordingly compelled to operate on two levels toward the Negro. In simplest terms, they are: (a) how he wants to act and (b) the discrepant way the other wants him to act. Spontaneity is impossible. The result is far from conversion, but it does mean the White is enacting the most basic theme in the life of the Negro. The continual guardedness; the conflict of an (a) and (b); the strain of having to act unnaturally: these are also the characteristics of the relationship that the Negro has traditionally had with Whites.

In short, the conversion to Blackness means learning proscriptions. The interdiction on the use of "nigger" is so cardinal that it is probably the first recognized by Whites. It is unlikely that any White has been granted a license by Negroes to use the term freely in addressing Negroes. Instead, the White looks for circumstances where his use of the term might be offset by the indirection. The standard case is where a White quotes a Negro whose comment included the word "nigger." A White student attending a Negro college only said "nigger" when referring to Negroes on the screen at campus films. He explained that celluloid Negroes were "removed . . . they couldn't retaliate."

Because the discovery of the ban comes early, the

White is more confused about rules covering its use late in his relationships with Negroes than he is toward the beginning. For the White may assume his conversion is so complete that no barriers exist. When one White, who thought he had reached this point of Blackness, used "nigger" he was told: "Listen man, you may be my good friend; but no White man can use that word to me."

The grounds for forbidding the use of "nigger" to Whites are best understood by looking at the basis for its acceptability when used by other Negroes. The term provides a democratic stigma—it applies to all Negroes equally. In that sense, any Negro using it is wounding himself as much as the intended recipient of the term. Historically, no Negro was exempted by Whites from qualifying as a "nigger." Negroes, in reciprocally drawing lines, have refused to exempt any White from the onus for the term. In using "nigger," the White is considered immune to the wound inflicted on Negroes: "You don't know how it feels to be called 'nigger.'"

If this explains why Negroes have the impunity to use "nigger," it does not explain why they use the term. Except for the upper strata (where race is effectively neutralized), "nigger" is commonly used among Negroes; among Negro civil rights workers it is used with the frequency of, and often in place of, punctuation. Because of the mutual injury, its use provides a reminder of their common enemy. The reminder, like the mutuality of the injury, acts as a bond of solidarity. The utility and satisfaction of this bond converts a negative term into a positive one. This conversion means that the bond is further strengthened, because the usage signifies a conquest of the enemy whose weapon has been turned against him.

Additionally, when Negroes use the term among themselves, the effect on the Movement White is something like the effect on the Negro when used by Whites. Since the term reminds Whites that it is forbidden to them, "nigger" (and equivalent terms, such as "boy," that are used, and not used, in the same way) gives them a sense of place.

Whites are more troubled by areas that are less obviously forbidden. Nothing is more apparently good-natured than joshing. But this is without seeing it as the Negro does. He sometimes refers to joshing as "joaning"; since the White finally regards joshing from the Negro point of view, it will be referred to here as joaning.

Because of its good-natured aspect, joaning usually has reverse elements. The White uses the joan to demonstrate that he feels comfortable enough with race to make light of it. That is to say, he offers it as a mark of what he regards as his conversion. He is, then, using a comic means to make a serious point. The mixture of these elements is emphasized when it is the specific content of the joan that is aimed at establishing the conversion; here, the statements that comprise the joan are presented whimsically, yet are meant to specify the grounds that led to the conversion.

Consequently, as seen in the letter that was sent to one of the Negro officers of a civil rights organization by a White staff member, the joan is liberating:

> Dear ———,
> Please place my name in the white box as a candidate for the trip to the Soviet Union. I was not at the staff meeting where the trip was discussed. However, according to [others in his project] who were there it was stipulated that of the group of four, at least two must be Negro. When I asked if there was also a stipulation that at least two of the sojourners be white, I was told that there was no such stipulation.
> These conditions being so I would like to make a couple of suggestions. First of all at the meeting at which people are selected, I would suggest that you

have two boxes, one of them labeled white and the other colored. Secondly, since the odds seem to be stacked in favor of that species heretofore described as Negro, I would like to be considered Negro for the purpose of this contest.

Yours in Freedom and Equality,

He begins by indicating (via the relevant box) that he is White. He goes on to explain his reference to the different boxes, and in so doing establishes himself as more extreme, or Blacker, than those Negroes who proposed the original method for selecting names. Since the Negro here is in an ascendant position, it is appropriate that the White should establish his claim on ascendancy, i.e., becoming a Negro, by using a technique, such as separate-but-equal, that is characteristic of Whites who are more avowedly ascendant than those who impose quotas. Therefore, at the end of the letter he suggests he has received the ultimate liberation by offering himself as a Negro.

But the White is not always able to engage in joaning unilaterally, as this letter permits. In face-to-face contact, the White discovers that it is not sufficient for him to believe he is entitled to joan. After a White teacher announced the date of an examination, a student explained why it was inappropriate. The teacher agreed: "That does seem to discriminate against you; there'll be no discrimination in this class." In trying to understand the incident, he recalled, "If I had to admit it, I was half-joking . . . I thought it was funny." But none of the students laughed. As a result, "After I said it, I thought: 'Oh, my God, what have I done?' I wasn't thinking. Next time, I'd think. I'd never say it again." So long as the Negro does not agree the White is entitled to joaning, it cannot succeed.

When a White is "half-joking," the Negro is more concerned with the other half. The following is how a student described the attempt of a White teacher to joan about the talk given at their college by a Nation of Islam minister who argued against Negroes using texts written by Whites, which he analogized to cats writing texts for dogs:

> After the lecture by [the Muslim] my English class under ———— had a discussion on the lecture. During this discussion my beliefs about [the White teacher] were confirmed. During previous class sessions I had gathered that ———— felt herself superior to us; not as a teacher might feel to a student, but as a White person to a Negro. She did this by trying to make us feel inferior. . . . After the lecture she stated her opinion of the speaker. She said that she thought most of his speech was "illogical," or "funny." She made a joke of the parable of the cat and dog education, and later called the [text used in their class] a "White man's book," referring again to the lecture. During her appraisal of the lecture she had this tone of voice that seemed to imply, "This man has come here and disturbed the minds of my students. I must give them the impression that they are getting a good break, and that they have no need to fight against the White man."

The Negro knows, from his own use of joaning, how much it conceals. He, too, has relied on the joan as an instrument for expressing feelings across racial lines. But any similarity to the use made of it by Whites does not extend to the content, insofar as it is derived by the Negro from his mistrust. Where the Negro feels a need to avoid an open break with the White, or, in any case, no need to induce one, but also wants to communicate his mistrust, joaning is useful. In the preceding stage, the White usually sees only the humor when joans are directed at himself; by the end of this stage, he sees only the seriousness. Upon getting into the car of a White volunteer, a Negro civil rights worker joaningly told about being shot at in Mississippi by a White driving a similar car. The Negro thereby indicated that the volunteer could just as well be the apocryphal racist. This interchangeability, however fanciful, was a reminder of where the White was in relation to trust.

The concealment possibilities of joaning also appear to the Negro through the various forms of liberation it has offered him. Considering the constraints traditionally imposed on his relations with Whites, nothing has been more liberating for the Negro than the outlet for aggression provided by "the dozens" (where each participant tries to outdo the other with humorously profane accusations about the other's mother). In this form, joaning reveals the thin line between comedy and brutality.

But there is another aspect of liberation through joaning for the Negro. It serves as a means of establishing contact with other Negroes. The parties involved in a successful joan celebrate it by slapping the hands of each other, so that the contact can be seen and heard. This gesture is described as "giving some skin," which is a statement of the unity that it represents. Joaning is itself probably a dialect version of joining.

By joaning, then, the White puts himself in a position where he is measured by a yardstick of aggression, or one of intimacy. Neither measurement is to the advantage of his conversion.

While all proscriptions weaken attempts at conversion, the most debilitating one is against being taken at face value. This rule is occasionally applied literally, as when a student said, "I wonder sometimes if behind that White smiling face and blue eyes [of the teacher], if there lies the thought: 'What am I doing here among all these niggers?' " More usually, it is the would-be beneficent acts of Whites that are seen through, and it is motives that are seen through the act. The conspicuousness of concealed motives was illustrated during a civil rights demonstration held on a campus. As reported by one student, when others noticed a White instructor participating, they began discussing what she was "doing here" in the march: "She loves us, and she's trying to prove it to us"; "She wants to be seen."[4]

The motive of another is relevant when his act is not considered an end in itself, but rather a means to an unknown end. The properties that Negroes implicitly ascribe to a motive assure its outweighing an otherwise acceptable act. The motive is the intent behind the act and the use to which the act will be put. The motive is a constant; it corresponds to what has occurred, is occurring, and will occur. The continuity provided by the motive in turn provides predictability. All of which assumes that, no matter how ill-conceived they are, motives represent the truth. As the source of actions, they are secluded to such an extent that deception would be unnecessary and is assumed, therefore, to not exist.

However, while using motives to establish the truth, Negroes are apt to have a set of relevant preconceptions. Traditionally, the conduct of the Negro in his relations with Whites has been calculated to give an appearance that reverses the underlying intentions. The Negro has therefore acquired an acute sense of the discrepancy between act and motive in matters of race. This perspective is facilitated by the legacy of false friendships received from Whites preceding the Movement; so that at the outset of the inspection, the mo-

---

[4] This reliance on motives is an alternative to the approach most often used by Negroes in the North to translate the acts of Whites. For the Northern Negro has access to a history of contact with Whites who approximate those in the Movement, allowing him to make the White Liberal, and his point of desertion, precisely documented and defined. Since it is assumed he will ultimately desert, all prior acts are simply moving the time closer, and therefore cannot be taken at face value.

By refusing to legitimize the motives of the White, Negroes in the South are asserting that he is acting beyond the limits of his dedication. Desertion is assumed to have *already* occurred.

tive of the Movement White is assumed to contradict his acts.

Outwardly benevolent acts by Whites become plausible when seen as disguising, hence inverting, the motive: domination of the Negro. Moreover, clinical proof does not exist for a motive; there is no objective truth that can dislodge a subjective interpretation of it. The interpretation is all the more durable when accompanied by a belief that there is nothing to be lost if wrong. Right or wrong, any other interpretation would mean a loss of control over what the White does with his act.

As a result of being preconceived, these motives become anthropomorphized. In one school, White faculty members are labelled by a generally known axiom as either "a misfit, a radical, or a missionary." There are variations in the alternatives from school to school, but the classification in some form is there as an initial assumption. A White was told by one of his students: "You're not an incompetent, and you don't look like a missionary. I'll have you bagged by next semester." The variety of categories reflects how long the college has had Whites on the faculty. "Radicals" originally referred to the refugees from Northern campuses who lost their jobs during the McCarthy period but found a sanctuary at Negro colleges, whose need for trained instructors overcame any political differences. At schools that did not have White faculty until recently, the only standardized analysis is "missionary," although the term is derived from the original White teachers who came South, following the Civil War, under the auspices of religious organizations.

If all the credentials of the White teacher are considered unsatisfactory, the students assume he is there because "he couldn't get a job anywhere else." When his credentials are more satisfactory, but lack teaching experience elsewhere, the motive shifts to: "He's just using [the College] as a stepping stone." Particularly when these credentials include experience, the White teacher is often asked the reason for his teaching there. An inference of the question was made clearer when a student phrased it this way: "You could have taught anywhere, why did you decide to teach here?" Students suppose the school is inferior to his qualifications, or at least that he considers it inferior. The qualification that most concerns them is race, which led one student to ask herself: "Why would they want to be Black?"[5] However, neither question causes them to suppose the White teacher is making a sacrifice by teaching there. As one student observed, "White folks ain't never done nothing unless they could get something out of it." The compensating factor is assumed to lie somewhere beneath the visible act of teaching; it can be found by uncovering the motive.

The search most often leads to the motive of paternalism. One Negro professor itemized the credentials of a White colleague and then asked, "Why would a man like that want to come to ———?" He went on to answer his own question: "He's trying to help us poor niggers." (Similar questions arise within civil rights organizations about White workers, since "you already have your rights"; similar answers are inferred.) Whites who know of this grievance continually insist on some version of "I'm certainly not in it to help the Negro, because I'm not paternalistic. I'm in it to help me." But this formula does not allow for the fact that paternalism is seen as a means of the White helping himself.

The act is aligned with the motive, and the motive is aligned with experience. Accordingly, paternalism is thought to provide its practitioner with a reward that, as one Negro

---

[5] The reference here is to Whites forsaking their world for that of the Negro. The reverse alternative is not often available to the Negro instructors, but when one of them who was teaching at a predominantly White university received an invitation to join a predominantly Negro college, he agreed—on the condition it provide his current salary plus an amount that he described as an "indemnity."

teacher noted about a White colleague, is "very necessary and essential to him." Further, this reward for the White is considered a penalty for the Negro. A student said, "I often get the feeling that White teachers are not in any way concerned with their Negro pupils being educated, but rather with the feeling of self-divinity they receive from helping the mental underdog."

Since his motive is questioned, or more precisely, challenged, the White cannot continue to take it for granted. Just as concern with the motive of someone else follows from and contributes to mistrust of him, so concern with one's own motive follows from and contributes to self-mistrust. As this search for a motive advances, so does self-mistrust.

Although Negroes regard motives as honest by definition, the imputation they usually give them can cause the White to falsify his motive. A White faculty member who disliked fraternities was asked to participate in the ceremony of one. The problem he realized a refusal would create was summarized by another White instructor whom he consulted: "It would never enter their heads that he was objecting to it because of principle . . . they would take it as a personal insult." The instructor started out with an anti-fraternity motive; his initial reaction was against participation. But he realized a refusal would be construed as the product of an anti-Negro motive. Subsequently, a new motive appeared— one based on acceptance seeking that results in an act opposite from his original motivation.

It is far easier to impute the motive of another than to introspect the motive of oneself. The imputation is guided by a monolithic viewpoint, while the introspection must survey and contend with a confusion of factors. The problem of isolating a single motive is all the greater when it must explain an act in which a broad area of the individual is invested. The diversity of motives that a White teacher perceives in himself is illustrated by the following extractions from a narrative describing one civil rights campaign:

> (a) . . . I am participating in this movement primarily because of my Christian beliefs.
>
> (b) My temptation is to participate in this movement for the increased prestige it will bring me among the people I work with.[6]

The identification of these motives was not guided entirely by introspection. A concern with the political reality was also at work. The relatively selfless explanation, (a), was given with Negroes present, whereas (b) arose with just the narrative present.

Usually, when there is an ideology such as (a), it is the only explanation acknowledged. Overarching conceptualizations simplify the basis for involvement. Moreover, they have an initial imperviousness to their inadequacy. Considerable insulation was provided for one White by his belief that he was teaching mathematics at a Negro college because "it was God's will." For it provides both a transcendent and portable ethos.

Eventually, the limitations of an ideology as motive appear. A civil rights worker, who is also a Marxist, was referring to the guilt feelings that he thought inhibited relations with Negroes when he explained, "I don't think you can get rid of them unless you begin thinking of it in class terms." With considerable reluctance, he further notes that class consciousness is rarely present in Negroes. A Negro civil rights worker, originally from the North, points out that "while the Whites factionalize themselves [into Marxist sects] . . . the Black people have got the foot on their neck." Further, Marx "never adddressed himself to the question of

---

[6] Merill Proudfoot, *Diary of a Sit-In*, Chapel Hill, The University of North Carolina Press, 1962, pp. 152, 32.

racism. He didn't write anything about the colonies of the European countries." Consequently, Marx appears to him as an illustration of the "White racist mentality."

This is not to say that where there is little market for an ideology it will be automatically abandoned by the ideologue. Exemptions are sought here too. Most ideologies have built-in explanations for an anticipated failure of their recruitment. In this way, it becomes not a failure, but a vindication of the ideology.

As a direct consequence of their various tactical advantages, ideologies provide the least effective rationale for participating in the Movement. Their self-sufficiency delays recognition of the effect they have, or do not have, on the Negro. Further, their simplicity leaves no room for deviation, either politically or spiritually—whichever is relevant. Their sanctity means that if deviation were possible, it would result in a moral crisis. Motives must be kept pure, and since the detailed criteria imposed by the ideology are met, it is believed they are pure, so that when the time is finally reached for self-examining motives, the collapse of belief is far more precipitous than in the case of the more flexible nonideologues.

The motive of a White appears less tenable as he becomes more attuned to the Negro. Ultimately, he finds himself without a motive. A White student at a Negro college told the students who asked why he transferred there: "I've always believed Whites and Negroes are the same, but I haven't known any. . . ." This was his reason until later that year when he realized, "I've changed so much since then. Now I don't know what my reason is."

Successive factors deprive the White of a motive. To begin with, he has discovered the unacceptability of his motive, or motives, to the Negro. A replacement is unavailable. For he also finds that the Negro does not have a motive that is transferable to Whites. Nor is the Negro willing to designate an acceptable motive. Finally, no motive of the White can be acceptable.

Applications to civil rights organizations require a statement of purpose which means, in effect, that the motive must be formalized. A Negro who helped assess over four hundred applications to a civil rights organization from Whites decided that none "were worth a damn." They usually wrote about " 'how they want to help the Negro and change the South'—a bunch of lies." Even more disturbing to him were those who did not lie. To illustrate, he described a hypothetical applicant "who said she had three years of college and could type 46½ words a minute. The worst part is when she gets down to the South. She comes into the Freedom House, and sees how she can make it immaculate . . . she also plans how she can run the office and doesn't want to go out to the field." A Negro administrator in another civil rights organization also found the White applicants wanting to uplift Negroes "like they are in some separate category— some kind of dog."

The main problem, for the White, is that Negroes do not need to offer a motive to each other. Their color suffices. The administrator cited one brief answer from a Negro that was, for her, overwhelmingly persuasive because it contained the phrase "I've been Black for a long time." She felt, "That tells a lot."

When race is involved, if Negroes look for motives in another Negro, it is ordinarily not to implicate, as happens to Whites, but to extenuate. He becomes an Uncle Tom (and, therefore, beyond extenuation) only when it cannot be established that his violating the interests of other Negroes resulted from coercion. The mechanics of extenuation are essentially no different from those of implication. In each case, the imputed motive establishes consistency between expectation and behavior where they might otherwise conflict.

A SUCCESSFUL CONVERSION
BY WHITES THAT IS SELF-DEFEATING

Through his contact with Movement Whites, the Negro acquires progressively more Blackness. Some of this additional Blackness takes the form of Negroes becoming White—while the White becomes a Negro, or more accurately considering his assigned place, a nigger.

Previously, Negroes could only become Whites in fantasy. Their enactment is still removed from the larger reality, but not the one of the Movement. A Negro civil rights worker from the rural South was trying to abduct a White volunteer while calling her "White girl" and explaining, "My boss-man told me to get you, and I'm going to get you." The circumstances are so inverted, that by orally and ostensibly emphasizing she is a White and he is a nigger, the opposite is actually emphasized.

While appearing to convert to Whiteness, the Negro is to a greater extent converting the Whiteness. A Negro civil rights worker said to a White participant: "I've seen you somewhere. Weren't you at the last Klan meeting I was at? Let's lynch him!" He refers to attending a Klan meeting and orders a lynching, but he is doing so as a Negro. The invented Klansman is to be punished by, rather than rewarded with, a lynching. Generally, where the Negro does act like a White, he is transforming the guidelines provided by those who once caused him or an acquaintance to act like a nigger. A White civil rights worker was told by a Negro co-worker, who was pointing a shotgun at him, to "get away from that colored woman." Later, by way of accounting for his rage, the Negro catalogued the injustices that his friends had been subjected to "over White women."

The Whites are not simply subjected to being niggers, they subject themselves to it. Before they contribute to the process, however, it is necessary to progress through the earlier stages. One of the first meals that a White civil rights worker ate in the South was at a restaurant operated by Negroes where he was not served until the Negro customers who came in after him had been; throughout the meal he was treated in a manner that led him to recall, "I was mad." He returned to eat there when his indignation gave way to a decision that the service he received, or did not receive, "is my people's fault." Considerations of a more tactical nature are also involved: Whites encourage their conversion to niggers, because it is the only one that Negroes make available to them.

With this accommodation goes an attempt to conceal skills that might be construed as inconsistent with subordination. A White was convinced that the civil rights office where he worked "needed reorganization terribly"; but rather than make suggestions based on considerable managerial experience, "I exposed my circles of ignorance." Self-denial becomes the means of acquiring and maintaining what is intended as fulfillment.

The extent to which Whites prostrate themselves was suggested by the figure of speech that one civil rights worker used to describe how he and other Whites in the organization responded to the open mistrust of their Negro co-workers: "We've sort of laid down and let them run over us." The policy of another White, at staff meetings, was "not to talk until I've understood what everyone has to say." In addition, "I left their black women alone."

Beyond not doing what others wanted to do (specifically, Negro males vis-à-vis Negro women), he "did what no one else wanted to do" (specifically, locating an area of work within the organization). For the passivity is not always by omission. A Negro officer of a civil rights organization is on unusually close terms with a White worker whom he calls "my nigger." The White calls him "my white man." In the course of washing dishes at a civil rights headquarters, a White organizer asked permission to take away the plate of a Negro organizer; when it was granted he said to the Negro, while bowing: "Thank you, Missa Cap'in." And a White teacher brought several members of his classes to a civil rights conference, attended mainly by Negro students, where he found an alternative to both his race and occupation by introducing himself at one of the workshops in this way: "I drove the car."[7]

The White also becomes a nigger in an effort to keep the Negro from becoming or remaining one. A White cleaned the toilet of a civil rights organization because he was afraid the Negroes working there "might think it was degrading." The White has moved beyond simply abandoning racial emoluments (intended for Whites); he is now acquiring racial penalties (intended for Negroes), and providing the Negro with the abandoned emoluments.

Throughout, the Negro expedites this downgrading of the White that results in the upgrading of himself. A Negro civil rights worker who, with her husband and child, shared an apartment with a White family from the same organization, announced that while waxing the floor she had been laughed at by the White husband, and consequently "I haven't waxed since. I'm not going to be anybody's nigger." The White husband, in describing the episode, insists, "I told her what I tell everyone: that after I got out of the Army I wasn't going to wax any more floors. It's a standard joke—I

---

[7] Institutions can become niggers as well. A White volunteer discovered this when asked by a Negro in a civil rights office whether certain items had been "sent to the campuses." Upon replying they were "sent to the Northern campuses," she was told: "They're not campuses, they're support groups." Campuses are where the organizing takes place. This distinction carries over to chapters of the group that are located in the North; their purpose is to "keep the Northern 'supply lines' open." As a result, according to official policy: "The only thing that we ask is that [the Northern chapters] stick to fund raising, political support and education. [They] are not to take local direct action in [the organization's] name."

was just bullshitting." But the interpretation of the Negro wife prevailed. Although she had just had a child of her own, the White wife found herself regularly washing dishes and babysitting for her opposite number. Like all Whites who have converted to niggers, she found herself as far removed from the Negro in this subordinate position as when she was in a superordinate position.

NEGROES ARE FREED
FROM THEIR ATTEMPTED CONVERSION

Movement Whites have been as successful in helping the Negro to acquire Blackness as they have failed in their own efforts at acquiring it. Besides being a target of the Negro's race consciousness, they are a source of it. For they are among those Whites from whom the Negro learns Blackness. A Negro told his audience of Whites, "I don't know what you expect from us, but I know what we expect from you—control." Another civil rights worker who is frequently told by Whites visiting his office for the first time, "I'm not aware you're a Negro," replies: "You're denying me something that I am; something that you created." In these cases, the Negro is including the White civil rights activist to stress the fact that he is indistinguishable from the racist. Yet, in several respects the White activist has "created" Negroes, with whom he has come in contact, to a greater extent than any other White. Although never purposely, this White has compelled them to find new channels for Blackness, while often providing these channels.

But, before the Blackness could be mobilized, Negroes, assisted by Whites, have had to overcome such obstacles as a sought conversion to Whiteness undertaken before joining the Movement. The Whiteness referred to here is aimed at becoming White without the concomitant objective of Blackness that states Whites must become niggers. Although the process may start long before the Negro colleges that most have attended, it is rarely promoted with as much thoroughness as they encounter here. At a Negro college that contributed more activists to the Movement than any other school, the Whiteness criteria were controlling from the time of application: "You had to be light, and bright, and damn near White," according to one former student and current activist; "You had to pass the 'palm test' to get in" (this meant holding the palm next to the face, to make certain the latter was not darker than the lightly pigmented former). On entering the college, it was discovered: "They wouldn't dare have Blues there because the alumni would revolt." The constraints toward conversion to Whiteness are difficult to withstand, since most of the students in Negro colleges are from the first generation of their family to attend, and much depends on becoming part of such requirements—even where it means "they would deride the way their mother spoke." (An atmosphere of this kind stoutly resists change, yet there have been indications that the distance between college and organization is diminishing, largely through the help of White instructors whose presence offers proof that the colleges "use us against the people.")

After being part of this milieu, its priorities are not easily abandoned. One Negro civil rights worker noted another who is "brushing his hair all the time, because it's 'too nappy.'" This remark tells as much about the speaker as it does about the Negro cited; in being able to identify and discuss this concern with "good" hair, he reveals a detachment from it that he did not have earlier. A college graduate and veteran activist explained, "My Aunt used to bring a tambourine to church, and jump up and wave it when she got happy. I used to be ashamed of her. I'm not ashamed of her now."

Conversion to Blackness is, therefore, initially as easy for the White as it is difficult for the Negro. The White is not personally threatened by rural Negroes, but it takes a while for Negroes who attended college (or acquired its orientation by other means) to get over seeing their Aunt among them, or rather, to see their Aunt among them in positive terms. A parallel case is the Southern White who joined the Movement to work with rural Negroes but resists working with rural Whites, because "I had nothing when I came out of there, and I'm afraid if I go back in I'll lose [what has been acquired since]"; unlike the rural Negroes, the rural Whites were not sufficiently remote from her to invest with fantasies.

Ultimately, the conversion to Blackness is as difficult for the White as it is easy for the Negro, insofar as their objectives are at cross-purposes. The White is using Blackness in an attempt to get close to the Negro. The Negro is too, but in addition, he is propelled past his initial reservations about Blackness by a determination to use it as a means of getting further away from the White. Blackness provides the Negro with his only recourse for dealing with the White, who must therefore be kept from access to it.

The forms of Blackness have been dictated by the White. His participation has caused Negro civil rights workers to feel the lack of control that precipitates mistrust. These Negroes have responded with a sequence of maneuvers that accompanied the evolution, within the Movement, of a protest against exclusion from the White world into one of protest against inclusion in the White world. In the process, the Movement White supplanted the Southern White as the principal target. When a Negro discovered there were no Whites present in the lodging provided by a civil rights organization, he shouted "Freedom at last," for it is the Movement White who has come to represent the coordinates by which the Negro locates his place.

(In what follows, no distinction is made between the effect that the various phases of these evolving tactics had on the White, because, although they unavoidably accelerated the recognition of mistrust, the mistrust was changing

in its degree of audibility and visibility, not in its nature—
nor in the nature of its effect on the White. Before procedures
for controlling Whites were fully developed, it was easier to
sustain what one former White activist has called "a naïve
brotherhood"; but there were unofficial intrusions upon it, as
seen in this section from a memorandum by another early
White: "If we are building in our own movement that be-
loved community, then race cannot be used to automatically
disqualify the argument of a white field secretary when policy matters are being discussed amongst ourselves.")

As viewed by Negroes, Whites try to impose their
strengths on the organization; the Negro has therefore tried
to adjust the organization to minimizing the strengths of the
White. The emphasis on "freedom organizations" is an example. The theory behind them is that to the extent the local
people are influenced by the organizer, they are also being
manipulated. It has been described by Whites as "participatory democracy," but the phrase intellectualizes the process
and thereby defeats one of its objectives, since intellectualiz-
ing is considered one of the unfair advantages of White organizers. Mainly Whites borrowed the concept from a White
student political organization and fit it to their argument for
more staff control over policy making. When later applied to
indigenous populations, it provided a means of defining and
limiting the place of Whites in the Movement. For example,
"participatory democracy" has lent itself to an anti-intellectu-
alism aimed at disarming the White. In talking to a White,
a Negro civil rights worker discounted the usefulness of his
formal education and added, "Everything I remember I
learned from [Mississippi Negroes]." Another Negro demonstrated a broader use of "participatory democracy" for plac-
ing Whites when he spoke to a group of them; one wrote this
account:

> [The Negro's] speech came primarily, I believe, as
> an objection to our discussion which, at that point, was

assuming that we were going into a community to *give them something*. That is, our attitude resembled what is known historically as the "white man's burden." Which has been and still is characteristic of the opinion of the "western world," especially the white developed nations, toward the non-western world, especially the non-white underdeveloped nations. . . . In simple language, we were trying to decide for people whom we had never met what was their good. What we were doing, then was quite similar to what the southern planter is doing when he maintains that it is much better for Negroes not to vote because he knows how to take care of them, he knows what they really need, and how to make them happy. It was this assumption on our part of presuming to know what is best for others that [the Negro] challenged.

At the same time, Negroes tend to doubt whether it could be otherwise, that is, whether the White can avoid imposing his terms on the Negro community. During another civil rights conference, one White described how she regularly brought a bookmobile to rural Negroes in order to acquaint them with Negro history. A Negro then pointed out that in the rural area, "Negroes listen to their traditions and their lives expressed [through music] on records." Moreover, books in general, and in particular the way they presented Negroes, were shown to be unreal to the rural Negro. Ralph Bunche was cited as a figure who is beyond the reach of their world; instead, "Could you make the pimps the heroes of the books?" The deeper problem was stated by a second Negro: "When Whites come, they come to help—whether consciously or unconsciously; to bring up. Because that's the [White] society they relate to."

Further along, Negroes have maximized a weakness of the White through an African revival within the Movement. The White tends to renounce his past in order to purge himself of responsibility for what his race has done, as well as his own earlier thoughts and acts toward Negroes. Or he may seek an exemption from his past, as a Southern White civil rights worker did in an essay entitled "Toward A New South" that referred to "the Negroes, who had indirectly been responsible for the plight of the poor whites." These Negroes were slaves; their oppression of Whites occurred when

> Poor Whites were pushed back into the hills by the competition of slave labor. The slave-plantation economy absorbed available capital, preventing the growth of a rich manufacturing base which could provide employment for white workers.

If this attempt at an exemption had succeeded, it would still be a long way from providing the White with roots in the Negro community.

Roots, an undeniable proof of inclusion, are sought by a self-contradictory process, for the White seeks them in the present. Meantime, Negroes in the Movement have begun seeking them by recapturing their past, as in a memorandum on "Black Consciousness" which was introduced with this statement:

> Man has constantly searched for his past. For it is his past which he uses as a foundation for his present and future. "Rootlessness" which grows out of a lack of understanding and misinformation "strips him naked" by depriving him of an historical frame of reference that comes out of knowing that anthropologists have discovered a "Negroid" skull dating back to 600,000 B.C. in what may have been the "Garden of Eden" in the fertile valleys of Kenya in East Africa. . . .

The White is granted as little claim for sharing in the cultural expressions of Africa as in this genealogy. The declared purpose of Africanisms is "race pride"; although this is, as one document states, "positive," it invariably acquires a negative aspect when Whites are thought to be intruding upon it. In fact, the pride results, to some extent, from a conviction that the revival is a defiance of Whites. A Negro civil rights worker appeared one day in an African dress and explained, "Some people say niggers aren't supposed to identify with Africa." The aggressive covetousness that accompanies this newly acquired culture revealed itself when a White volunteer attended a party that was mainly comprised of Negro civil rights workers. They started doing an African dance, and she followed along on the side until one of the Negroes asked her whether she was an African; when she replied "No," he asked: "Then why are you dancing?" She left, and he followed after her, shouting, "I told you not to dance," as he shook his fist in her face. While the White impels these Africanisms as a challenge to his presence, their content, especially Négritude, provides further grounds for challenging him, in addition to preparing for the next technique.

A later (though, as all have been, overlapping) approach to Whites arose from a situation described by a Negro who has been close to the Movement since its inception: "As activists they [the Negroes] could outdo any White coming down, but they couldn't compete on their terms." The Negroes "felt inadequate in face of the Ivy Leaguers" who reversed the existing terms by imposing ones derived from "being articulate and conceptualizing."

These new terms were eventually adopted and adapted by Negroes, an increasing number of whom arrived from the North. Their Blackness had received its momentum from the civil rights activities of Southern Negroes, whose already present, but amorphous, mistrust these Northern Negroes were able to concretize into the highest form of articulation and conceptualization—an ideology, as in this excerpt from a memorandum:

> In an analysis of our history in this country, we have been forced to come to the conclusion that 400 years of oppression and slavery suffered in this country

by our Black forebears parallels in a very graphic way
the oppression and colonization suffered by the African
people. . . . When it comes to the question of organizing Black people, we must insist that the people who
come in contact with the Black masses are not white
people who, no matter what their liberal leaning is, are
not equipped to dispel the myths of western superiority. White people only serve to perpetuate these myths;
rather, organizing must be done by Black people [who]
are able to see the beauty of themselves, are able to
see the important cultural contributions of Afro-Amer-
icans, are able to see that this country was built upon
the blood and backs of our Black ancestors.

The increasingly well-formulated danger embodied by
Whites surpassed any safeguard except a prohibition against
their working in Negro communities. Even this one was soon
considered inadequate. The final prohibition was against
Whites remaining in the organization.

WHITES ARE FREED
FROM THEIR ATTEMPTED CONVERSION

One way of summarizing the internal obstacles on the way
to conversion is that the White can never become simply a
subject: one who sees the world as a Negro would. He must
also, when relevant, see himself as a Negro would a White;
in this way he becomes an object. In other words, although
his goal for conversion is to lose himself in Blackness, the
effect is for the White to keep closer track of his whereabouts
than before.

The eagerness of the White to achieve conversion ac-
celerates the self-objectification. In order to forget Whiteness, he reaches a point where, according to a White civil
rights worker, he is "trying so hard that it makes it impossible
to forget." In the process, he manages to remind the Negro

with equal forcefulness. While driving his car, a White teacher spent a considerable time trying to locate a station that played Negro music; after succeeding, he whistled along with it and repeatedly interrupted himself to remind his listener, "I've got soul." The Negro student who was his listener later stated her view of the proceedings: "I'd never work that hard."

Initially, the White consciousness that is prompted by self-objectification can be rendered painless by undertaking it within the terms of equivalence, during the later part of the exemption-seeking time period. It serves as another form of concession and, thereby, as another assist in the transition to mistrust recognition. The process frequently involves a return to the culture that the White had been born into, so that he has an unchallenged claim to membership in it, that is, a community where trust is not an issue.[8] Teachers, who had forsaken Judaism, suddenly find themselves reclaiming it; one of them decided that, for instance, his children should attend religious school. He considered himself to be acting in the same way that a civil rights worker, who appeared on campus, urged other Negroes to act when "he talked about the suppression of culture." (But, he rearrived at Judaism through the peculiarities of his situation, not through a commonality with Negroes. He had argued for the freedom of Negroes by opposing compulsory chapel, and in turn, was opposed by the Negro faculty and administration, to whom his argument "was just inconceivable." He suddenly saw it was a matter of what "battles you've fought," which meant he became aware of himself as a Jew, whose traditional battle

---

[8] The prior culture may also appear in an early aspect of exemption seeking, but then it takes the form of a past occurrence, and is introduced only for the purpose of showing that the White has served an apprenticeship as a Negro. As an example, Jews who recite their encounters with anti-Semitism in order to demonstrate they "know what it's like to be a Negro." However, the Negro is likely to see the Jew as more than, not less than, a White: "You know, the Jews try to take everything over." When later introduced, Judaism occurs in the present, and more for its own sake.

was what he described as "religious liberty.") An instructor who had earlier escaped his Irish origins to the extent of attending a Jewish college explained that his sudden purchases of books about the Irish Rebellion were the result of the same Negro "talking about roots." In these cases, the White consciousness was further facilitated by focusing on oneself as the member of a minority group; but it is, nonetheless, an acknowledgement of being a species within the White genus.

As self-objectification increases, so does White consciousness; as White consciousness increases, so does a disbelief in the mythology of a trust relationship with the Negro. This is the sequence that leads to the final recognition of mistrust, but when it is reached, the reverse process occurs. Mistrust is undeniably recognized, so that the White can see himself without disguise. For by completing the demolition of fantasies that expressed themselves through, and were preserved by, his now-leveled defenses, this recognition of mistrust leaves the White with an unobstructed, though desolate, view of himself.

He can now see the dimensions of the need he had all along for the trust of the Negro. This basic component of the contact, and of his being White, stands out in the greatest possible relief because it is discovered through the mistrust of the Negro—the other basic component of the contact, and of his being White. One White suggested the extent of his reliance on and rejection by the Negro when he described the discovery as having "pulled the pins out." At the time of her unstructuring discovery, another White said, "I just don't like feeling so unwanted. I feel like a bird in a nest that's being pushed out, and told: 'Go fly.'"

In trying to cope with this discovery of mistrust, the White may well become still more conscious of his Whiteness. A White civil rights worker found himself regularly visiting the apartment of a White female civil rights worker "for what I call 'a White evening': We'd have tuna casserole, listen to some records, discuss a few books, and salve our racial wounds."

Here the White is undergoing a disengagement from Negroes that typically follows the discovery of mistrust. For a different reason, disengagement often occurs in the preceding stage. This earlier disengagement is limited, and intended to demonstrate an exemption from Whiteness based on an unwillingness to dominate. The two varieties of disengagement appear in the adjustments made by a White whose civil rights career in the South began with the administration of a Freedom School. His experiences led him to formulate a new project for the following summer: again working in Mississippi, but this time with two Negroes who would do the organizing, while he did the research for them. That is, his place was to be one where he provided no more than services to Negroes; it was disengagement through subservience. His plans were changed by further experiences during the year; the most decisive one occurred at a civil rights conference of Negro college students. After a Negro speaker referred to the implantation of racial "understanding" in the Negro masses, this White said: "I'd just like to ask one question: How do you reach that understanding?" The Negro replied: "One thing that disturbs me here is that we have people, forces, here who are not in our family." The White thereupon reported feeling the full weight of the mistrust. (The recognition can be delayed when it has not been cumulative: a similar resistance was encountered at a meeting by a recently arrived White exchange student who saw it as evidence that the Negroes were not against Whites, but rather against discovering that Whites were acceptable, for "They felt the validity of their clichés [about Whites] threatened.") After his cumulative discovery, the White decided to absent himself from the remaining session. One of those he spoke to was a White student at a Negro college who agreed: "If I hadn't

been White, I would've suggested it myself at the meeting."
The reason he later gave for his reticence made it more explicit that he, unlike the other White, had not completed the
transition to the present stage, for the earlier form of disengagement was stated: "Whites shouldn't say anything that
affects policy." In urging others to join him, the initiator of the
withdrawal explained, "People don't feel free to talk" (his reference was not to the accusing Negro, a Northern organizer
who was patently uninhibited, but to the Southern students
who had not spoken); consequently, "The presence of Whites
is affecting the color and complexion of the discussion." Instead of Mississippi, he decided to spend the summer in
Europe.

In short, when the White discovers that he cannot
withdraw from his Whiteness by converting to Blackness, he
withdraws from Negroes. A White teacher who had not hesitated to introduce racial material into his English class found
himself dreading an announced class discussion of an assignment that dealt with race. The assignment and announced
discussion were no different than many that had preceded it,
but the teacher was different. He had discovered that he was
not, after all, exempt from the mistrust of his students. As a
result, he was saying: "I have less and less courage about
these things." But it was only in retrospect that "courage"
was necessary. While formerly pursuing racial topics, it had
not seemed courageous because he assumed his trustworthiness was, at worst, negotiable. Now he wanted to avoid at
all costs having to discuss the reading that he had been looking forward to. Besides now realizing how vulnerable he was,
the teacher feared that if he followed the procedure that had
become customary in his classroom, it would have no success
—a possibility that he had never considered before. Consequently, he decided that rather than lead the discussion, he
would have no part in it. He appointed a panel of students to
discuss it: "I thought if I asked questions they'd clam up. But

if they asked each other questions they might discuss it among themselves."

No aspect of the relationship, or would-be-relationship, with Negroes is free of reassessments. When he first arrived, a White teacher did not hesitate to sit with his White colleagues. About a year later he said: "I don't like it when Whites cluster together at meetings and in the cafeteria. It's bad." (The White students whose main concern was, say, the School of Veterinary Medicine, not Negroes, were easily identifiable in the cafeteria because they sat together; if they tried to join a Movement-oriented White, he would immediately move away, rather than have it thought that Whites claimed him as their own.) The teacher realized that if Whites were going to sit with their colleagues in the cafeteria they had no choice, since Negro faculty did not eat there. But "I can't see it that way . . . because the students don't see it that way." He carried it still further: "They have very little self-respect. It affects the way they think about themselves. They think the Whites don't want to eat with them. You know, eating is a very intimate act in the South." The White teacher had already "tried sitting down next to a student. He didn't know what to do. He soon got up and left. It wasn't as though I had singled him out . . . there was a place next to him so I sat down." The remedy he eventually chose was purchasing a sandwich in the cafeteria and then eating it alone in his office.

These various styles of disengagement, occurring in this stage, also serve as a means of phasing out from the Movement. The interval between recognizing an unsuccessful conversion and the ultimate disengagement—the return North—varies considerably. Civil rights workers do not usually have access to a cushioning "White evening." Their departure is more likely to be abrupt, as in the case of a White who left the South because "I'm not that important that I should cause all these problems. The best thing I can do is just leave." Faculty members are, of course, bound by contract to finish their year. Meantime, they withdraw from all forms of exposure, such as the after-hours seminar and other exemption apparatuses, upon deciding that, for instance, "What this place needs more than White faculty is administration reform, and maybe we're just making them entrench themselves." (This teacher initially considered race to be an irrelevant characteristic of teachers; the fact that more Whites were involved in campus causes was attributed to an age difference: he noted that Whites were generally young, and young Negro instructors had, in his view, these same enthusiasms. As an example, one of the young Negroes advocated the repeal of R.O.T.C. Eventually, however, the White discovered that the Negro had been "more successful" than he in winning student allies for the war against R.O.T.C. (In fact, the White concluded that among his students, "The apathetic ones became more apathetic and the resistant became more resistant.")

These Whites have discovered that conversion for them is a contradiction in terms. The effect of this discovery accounts for a Negro student observing, "Most White teachers come with the feeling they're God or Jesus, but after a while they become adjusted." Actually, the extraterrestrial viewpoint of the teacher means that he feels adjusted at the outset. When he adjusts to the outlook of the student, by discovering he is seen as a self-appointed God, he feels profoundly unadjusted. For in the process, these Whites have moved to the other extreme from the early stages where mistrust supposedly did not exist, or later, where it did not have enough relevance to offset their supposed contributions. As it now appears to them, so far from making overriding contributions, they have been undermining the Movement. They are, at last, able to "think Black."